BREAKTHROUGH COPYWRITING

HOW TO GENERATE QUICK CASH WITH THE WRITTEN WORD

DAVID GARFINKEL

Copyright Notice

Published under the Copyright Laws of the Library of Congress Of The United States of America, by:

The World Copywriting Institute
A division of David Garfinkel, LLC
236 West Portal Ave., #255
San Francisco, CA 94127

Publisher's Advisory: Copy is powerful. You're responsible for how you use what you read in this book. Most of the time, common sense is all you need. But if you make extreme claims... and/or if you're writing copy for offers in highly regulated industries like health, finance, and business opportunity... you may want to get a legal review after you write and before you start using your copy. David's larger clients do this all the time.

ISBN-13: 978-1548706951
ISBN-10: 1548706957

CONTENTS

FOREWORD

My name is Bond Halbert and if you spend any time in the world of direct marketing, you probably recognize my last name because my father was one of history's greatest copywriters, Gary C. Halbert. But... that's not the reason you should hark unto me.

Having a highly successful or famous/infamous father is just a matter of dumb luck. But there is a very solid reason to take my word for what I'm about to tell you.

You see, my father lived, ate and breathed copywriting to such an extent, that most of our everyday father-son talks were about marketing and then my training was put on steroids when my father singled me out to be mentored.

Soon and long before I was old enough to drive, I was not only privy to high level marketing meetings, but I was participating as well and I have had a long fruitful career myself. I'm not telling you this to brag. I'm explaining this so you will understand that almost nobody has been around as many top copywriters and copy cubs learning to write ads as I have.

I get asked all the time about the best ways to learn copywriting and I believe the best course of action depends upon your final goal. To write effective copy really frigging fast, I recommend the services of Mr. David Garfinkel.

You see, David has spent an epic amount of time boiling down the hard earned lessons of his uber-successful copywriting career and the lessons of the masters who showed him the way, into a system or way of thinking, specifically designed to take a complete newbie and get them up and writing profitable money-making ads very, very fast.

The book reads like someone managed to convince Mr. Garfinkel to share his best ideas, and that conversation was then translated into Breakthrough Copywriting — which actually makes this so very cool.

Whenever even veteran copywriters write about their craft, it takes them forever to get to the point. Because they usually worry too much about some troll parsing their words and this makes for a really boring read but not so here.

This is like eavesdropping on a marketing wizard's candid conversation about what it takes to write winning ads.

It's not polished, because it's raw, fast and honest or what we in the business call "the down and dirty."

All the key concepts are trimmed to make this a super fast read, which is like a cheat sheet reminding you of the most important concepts in making sales and creating the kind of direct response promotions proven to be money-making machines for copywriters and their clients.

Sir Bond of Halbert

INTRODUCTION

I wrote this book with one purpose: *to get you from wherever you are now, to wherever you want to be, in regard to attracting business and closing sales with the written word.*

This book is probably different than any other you have read because of the urgency. All my life I have felt urgency. Literally, all my life. As a little boy, I was nicknamed "Instant Coffee" by my parents because I had no patience and wanted everything *now*.

I soon came to realize I was unusual in this regard.

You see, most people would prefer a world without urgency, where there is enough time to think things through and do what you have to do without any stress.

That would be nice!

But in the words of Robert Ringer, in his book *Action! Nothing Happens Until Something Moves*:

"A stress-free life sounds nice in theory, but in reality there is an inherent urgency to life. For one thing, life is finite, and you don't even have the advantage of knowing when your finite supply of time will run out.

"Second, life is competition. No matter what your situation, you're already competing with other human beings. You compete for a prospective spouse, you compete for a place on an athletic team, you compete for attention from others, you constantly compete in ways you don't even think about.

"If you don't want the competition to leave you in the dust, you can't coast. You've got to take positive action and make progress every day of your life."

Today, if we spent some time together in person, you very well might see me as one of the most patient people you ever met. What about the inherent urgency to life?

Learning patience has been a lifelong task for me. There's a paradox: You need to feel the urgency, but you need to live your life with genuine patience. To explore this requires a full-blown philosophical discussion; maybe my next book. :)

In any event…

So how does all this relate to copywriting?

That's easy. Even in the most patient person's world, life is primarily about action (I think it is).

And if life is primarily about action, then copywriting is the communications medium that prompts action in others (and this can be proven).

Therefore, the ability to write copy is very important.

In fact, writing copy is the number-one skill you need to take *real* control of your life, which is certainly not about micro-managing details or totally eliminating stress.

What copywriting is about: Options. Choices. Freedom. Being able to create written statements that will provide you all sorts of things — money, free time, agreement from others, access to people you could not have gotten otherwise — so that you have a greater degree of control over your life than you ever dreamed possible.

Of course copywriting also has some nuts-and-bolts, down-to-earth, practical benefits:

- You can start a business from scratch, with no investors, and generate enough cash-flow so you can grow the business with sales alone, and keep full ownership
- You can get more customers for your existing business
- You can get paid very well to write copy for others
- You can become a generally more persuasive person in all aspects of your life.

As Bond Halbert pointed out in his foreword, I get right to the point.

I would agree.

So let's get started.

David Garfinkel
San Francisco

1

THE FOUR ADVANTAGES OF BREAKTHROUGH COPYWRITING

Copywriting is about communicating with the *emotional* part of a person's mind in a way that makes sense to the *rational* mind. The emotional part of your mind is called your unconscious mind.

Within everyone's unconscious mind, there's a place called "Copywriting Junction." It's the intersection of a road we're on.

One side says, "No." On the other side, it says, "Yes."

On another road, on one side it says, "Bad," and on the other side, it says, "Good."

At the intersection is the place called "Maybe."

When people see your sales letter, VSL, copy, email, or Google AdWords, they are in a condition of "maybe." Your job with copy is to get your prospect through the intersection and onto the side of the road that says, "Yes."

The Breakthrough Copywriting Model is designed to help you do just this. It is unique because it covers skills and tools in four areas:

1. Thinking is vitally important. But this is also what you learn from virtually every other copywriting book or seminar.
2. Feeling involves how you are able to convey passion and other feelings effectively in your writing, so you're not writing about them. People are getting what you are feeling, or what you're trying to make them feel, from your words.
3. Insight involves intuition and the ability to take your intuitive thoughts, feelings, impulses, and images of that information and turn it into a conclusion, a direction, an action, a map, or a pathway. Insight is about using your intuition to make money.
4. Energy level means *your* energy level — how excited you are. That energy can be poured into the written word. It's in the energy of the writing, the rhythm, the power, and the passion.

Before we start, let me tell you what most people seem to go through with copywriting and even what I went through, even though I had many years of experience as a professional writer. It's a long tedious struggle — lots of errors. Lots of paths you go down that don't seem to work. Maybe this has been your experience, too.

Even when you're very experienced and very good, it probably takes a lot of time for you no matter what level of experience you have. I think you're going to find this book is going to make it easier for you to write copy. It will probably save you a lot of time. And certainly, it will help improve your results.

There is an old definition of copywriting that says, "Copywriting is salesmanship in print." That is valid to a degree. Although, it does exclude about half of the earth's population who are women. Also, it's not realistic from a technical point of view.

So, I've come up with a 21st century definition of copywriting that I would like to share with you. Copywriting is using the written word to start, enhance or extend a relationship with a customer that subsumes, or includes, salesmanship in print. That could be one of the things, but it's not the only thing.

Have you ever stopped to think about how many steps you went through before you made a purchasing decision and paid money for something? You may have responded to an email from somebody. It could have been one of many emails you received from that person. Then, you may have gone to a website.

Even when it came to purchasing this book, you went through a decision process. You may have known instantly that you wanted to buy this book because you were familiar with my work and me. You may have read the book's description. You may have taken a look at the reviews posted about the book. You may have even been in that middle place called "maybe." A number of things happened which got you here. We're going to talk about that because you can do the same thing for your customers.

It's really important to understand that you do not know what your sales process is until you've tested it, or until you've tried at least a few different things. The real money in copywriting is understanding all of these things and then testing one element against another until you find the optimal way.

Many of the most successful sales letters — ones that have brought in a million dollars or more in a single day — had a lot of steps that went ahead of it that were significant. Now, without a good sales letter, it wouldn't have happened. But the sales letter was the gateway and the final push of a carefully thought out, articulated process.

We'll discuss this further throughout this book. The key to defining the steps you have is to know what action you are asking the reader for, and to know what result you are going to get. Where are they going to be in the process? Of course, the better a person knows you, feels they know you, or knows about you, the easier it is to get them to go through your steps.

And, it's something you do *for* your customers and not *to* your customers.

There are different ways of looking at copywriting. I'm going to tell you mine. The Breakthrough Copywriting model is different from any other I've seen. I invented it because I looked at people I had mentored — some of them have become raging successes; some of them have become disappointing failures.

I looked at what the difference was. It wasn't intelligence. It wasn't education. It wasn't even motivation. I know if I were a motivational speaker, I would tell you if they just got motivated, then they would get it done. But, that is not my conclusion.

My conclusion is that they took in the knowledge, but there were things holding them back. Breakthrough Copywriting is designed to help get people past those things that are holding them back.

The Breakthrough Copywriting model covers four things. Thinking is what you learn at other copywriting seminar or in copywriting books. Most of the thinking you learn at most copywriting seminars and in most copywriting books is not that good. Even though you can sometimes learn very good thinking with some books and at some seminars, it's not enough. It's not enough to help you cross that line between writing copy that is okay and copy that is exceptional.

I don't believe anyone else has really taught the other three things that help make the difference between copywriters of average ability and copywriters of exceptional ability.

Just to be very specific about this — the strategies, the techniques, the test results, and the positioning — all of those things involve thinking, knowledge, mind work, and mindset. Those are extremely important. But, there are three other parts that could be what is holding you back. These are feeling, insight, and energy.

With feeling, it is not just about getting in touch with your feelings. Feeling involves being able to convey passion and other feelings effectively in your writing. When this is done effectively, you don't have to write about your feelings. People are getting what you're feeling. They are getting what you're trying to make them feel. They feel it themselves.

Now, how do you do that? You do that by getting in touch with your unconscious mind. Fear and blocks are what may be preventing you from being able to do this.

The third component of the Breakthrough Copywriting approach has to do with insight. Insight involves intuition and the ability to take your intuitive thoughts, feelings, impulses, and images and turn that information into a conclusion, a direction, an action, a map, or a pathway.

This is especially important in copywriting in a couple of areas. One is the area of strategies. The other is the area of markets. Strategies are the ideas you're going to use that are going to work and make you money. Markets have to do with who the prospect is, and just as importantly, who the prospect is not. That is, knowing who is the ideal person and understanding what are they are feeling.

It's important to keep in mind that copy is not the kind of writing you learned in school. Copy is the spoken language in written form. You're having dialogue. It's like a personal letter to somebody. If you don't know who that person is, how can you get personal? You end up writing a generic letter.

How much money do people make with generic copy? Millions and millions of dollars. The people who make that are the advertising agencies who get 15% of the amount the newspaper charges, or the TV network charges to run the ad. But, the business owner doesn't make much money with generic copy.

Insight is the ability to use your intuition to make money.

Then, there is energy. Energy means two things. Energy means your energy level — how excited you are. Energy also means energy that can also be poured into the written word. If you've read copy that is sizzling with energy, you know exactly what I'm talking about. So, that's one thing about energy. It's the energy of the writing, the rhythm, the passion, and the power.

The other thing about energy is your energy level. Have you noticed that copywriting can be exhausting? Yes, it can be. There are two elements of personal energy I'd like to talk about. One is what blocks get in the way and what that does to your energy. When you are blocked, it can make you feel tired. It can make you procrastinate. It'll make you lazy. It'll make you distracted.

The other thing is biochemical. You don't want to write copy after you've eaten a heavy Italian meal. It's okay to eat heavy Italian meals after you've written the copy.

So, that's what Breakthrough Copywriting is about.

Ted Cooper is a fellow copywriter living just down the San Francisco Peninsula from me. He is one of the few copywriters I know who successfully broke through into corporate marketing and was able to continue to do direct-response copy. He wrote ads that started Intuit, which makes Quicken and QuickBooks, and he wrote ads that started Apple. He really built up those companies with his ads.

He says that his formula — and this will set the context for what I'm going to tell you — is #1 make a promise, #2 prove it, and #3 ask for action.

This fourth step I'm about to give you is really important. Leave everything else out. That means that copy is very intentional and is very focused on getting an action from the person reading it. While that action could be a sale, it doesn't have to be. It could be getting someone to opt-in to your mailing list. It could be getting somebody to complete a reply card. Or, it could be some other type of action.

Traditional institutional advertising — the kind you used to see before you knew about copywriting and the kind you see in magazines — is sort of called "Freudian advertising." They're concerned about what you *think*, similar to, "Oh, what are you thinking about me?" It's like Sally Field saying, "Oh, you like me. You really like me." That isn't going to make any sales, but it might help you in a popularity contest or win a poll where your recognition or popularity is higher. But, your banker doesn't care. You might care, but it's not going to help your business too much.

Direct response copy has been described as Skinnerian or behaviorist. That means we don't really care what you *think*. But, we do care about what you *do*. We don't care if you like us as long as you buy from us. We don't care if you hold us in the highest esteem as long as you become a customer and you're satisfied.

That is the mindset of a direct response copywriter. It is very different from what they teach you in school, and it's very different from the mindset of most of the mass media. It is also different than the conditioning, the folkways and mores of our society. And, it is what is going to make your world go around once you start getting the gist of this stuff.

Let me tell you about the anatomy of a sales message from my point of view. You start with a headline. Have you ever spent a week or more writing a headline? I'm going to show you how to write a good headline in about sixty seconds, later in this book.

A headline and a compelling opening sentence are 80% of the

sale. There is a saying from legendary copywriter Gene Schwartz that the purpose of a headline is to get you to read the first sentence. The purpose of the first sentence is to get you to read the second sentence. If you can get them to read about three or four sentences, you have a very, very high chance they will keep reading the sales letter.

From there, you want to make an emotionally compelling case. An emotionally compelling case is something that reaches them in their gut, their stomach, their solar plexus, and their heart. The one response you don't want to get is, "Interesting idea. That's really good copy. You write well."

The response you want to get is either "We're going to get one of those," or "You can't do that!" You want to get them one way or the other. You want to get a negative reaction from the people your offer is not right for, and a positive reaction from the people who it is right for. And, that is what an emotionally compelling case does.

It also means that the people who are not in your target market are not going to get it. They are not going to understand it unless they are copywriters and they know how to adjust their minds in that particular way. So, it is a different way of looking at things.

What happens when you make an emotionally compelling case for the person who is actually a good prospect for you? You develop resistance. The more excitement you create, the more skepticism comes up on the other side. The more excitement you create and the better job you do with the emotionally compelling case, the more you are going to create resistance.

How do you combat this resistance in a way that the reasoning part of the mind can accept? You do this with factual backup. We'll be covering all of these things in detail. I'm trying to give you the big picture before we jump into a lot of detail.

From there, you create an offer. An offer is not what you are selling. It is a way of presenting the benefits and the features, or aspects of what you're selling in a way that is so compelling that it is easier to say "yes" than to say "no." The last part is to ask for a specific action and clearly spell out the steps in ways you might think are blatantly or even insultingly direct.

I got a postcard once from a sales training company. They said that 82% of sales people, professional sales people, do not close. Why? Because they do not ask for the order. They do not request action.

I have a friend named Ben Gay who published a book called *The Closers*, which is a real hard-core, nitty-gritty, street-fighting book about sales. He also published a newsletter called *The Closers Newsletter*, and he wrote a second book called *The Closers II*. I asked him about the postcard. I said, "What do you think about that?"

He said, "I don't think that's right."

I said, "What do you mean?"

He replied, "I think that's too low."

(That means Ben thinks more than 82% of professional sales people do not close. They do not ask for the order. They do not request action.)

What is the problem with asking somebody to buy? For many

people, the problem is they might say "no." No copywriter really likes rejection. Maybe some people do, but most people don't.

The reason I bring this up is when you have a sales message and you have copy, you are putting this sales conversation in print or on the Internet. If you have trouble asking for action in person or asking for money, guess what? You are going to have trouble asking for it in copy, too. That is, if you're going to do it with real passion, force, commitment, and intention.

But, you can get the courage to do it. Courage doesn't mean absence of fear. Courage means action in the face of fear. When you get the courage to do that, you will be able to ask for the sale or ask your prospect to take an action better.

So, how did I get here? In 1987, I took some sales training from a very interesting fellow, Jim Camp. Jim was a world-famous negotiation coach. My training with Jim was the very beginning of this.

From there, a couple of years later, I co-authored a book on sales management. I noticed this guy who had been the top salesperson for five years at a Fortune 500 company didn't sell at all. All he did was get on the phone, talk to his customers, make special deals for them, make them feel comfy and happy, and then ask them for referrals. He got referrals, and he got more referrals. He didn't work all day; he worked maybe half a day. But, he was incredibly good at just making people feel comfortable, having connections with people, and continuing to get referrals.

I thought that was the answer. I hadn't learned the difference between want and need yet. I found out you can make a fortune selling people what they want, but you can go broke selling them what they need.

I learned that the hard way when I took the wrong path down the road. I went broke selling people what they needed. I put together a course on referrals. Maybe you know about it. It's called Referral Magic: 17 Ways to Let Your Clients Do Your Selling. It's a great tape. I had a vision that didn't quite come to pass with it, though. I thought everyone was going to realize they needed this and would buy it. The margin was pretty good. I thought I would retire and ride off into the sunset. Well, I do live in a San Francisco neighborhood called The Sunset now. But that is the only thing that actually came true.

In the process, I found that the biggest problem I had was that I was trying to sell. I was trying to sell people something they needed rather than what they wanted. People didn't want to get this information — at least the way I was selling it. This was in the early 90's.

The other thing is, I didn't have any copywriting skills. Maybe it was that I didn't understand the copywriting skills I had. I think I actually had them, but I didn't know how to use them. And, because I wasn't presenting prospects with a clear picture of how buying my product would improve their lives and I was promising something most people didn't want, sales were very slow.

Later, I went to Gary Halbert's "Hurricane Andrew" seminar in Key West, Florida. That changed my life. Gary Halbert's seminar was interesting.

A few years later, I met Jay Conrad Levinson. He asked me to write a book with him. Jay's the author of the Guerrilla Marketing Series, which is the best selling series of marketing books in the world. Things started to go on an upward spiral, and things continued like that.

On April 11th, 2000, *Killer Copy Tactics* was released on the Internet. Mark Joyner took a course I had done the year before and digitized the audio. At the time, that was still pretty new. I think we made $60,000 in sales the first month. There were a couple of years in my life that I hadn't made $60,000 altogether, so this was pretty amazing.

At one point, I decided that I was going to teach people how to write copy. I became determined to be the best in the world at it, and I believe that I am. There are better copywriters than I am, but I will stake my claim as the best teacher. No one has successfully challenged me on that yet.

And, from this determination to be the world's best copywriting teacher, the strategies that make up Breakthrough Copywriting emerged.

2

HOW TO BUILD A MESSAGE THAT MAKES MONEY

When it comes to the kind of writing you're going to do when you write copy, everything you learned in school is wrong. In school, you were taught to be reactive. You were taught to be subservient. You were taught to be obedient or compliant. But you were not taught to be proactive. Being proactive could get you sent to the principal's office, right?

But copy is all about being proactive, so being proactive has an implication. The implication is that you're going to stir things up. You're going to provoke. And this goes against the very fiber of our beings as we were trained to be in school and possibly even in our families. But, as you may have noticed, the things that seem to work most of the time and in most situations are very proactive. They are very bold. One thing they all have in common is that they stir emotions.

Stephen Covey has a concept he talks about in *The Seven Habits of Highly Effective People*. He talks about the emotional bank account that you have in every relationship with every other person. With copy, each person also has sort of an emotional bank account. Maybe you would want to call it an emotional thermometer or an emotional barometer. When it gets above a certain pressure point, they go, "Yes, I want that."

I noticed that in myself when I was watching movie trailers. Sometimes I would see a trailer for a movie that I really wasn't interested in. About the 4th or the 5th time I saw it, suddenly it became more interesting to me more relevant, and something I wanted to see.

Has this ever happened to you? It's almost like there is this *click* that you hear in your brain. "Yeah, I've got to go see that movie." My emotional bank account, my emotional thermometer, my emotional barometer finally got to the point where my desire outweighed my resistance.

We want to do the same thing when we write copy. Unfortunately, with copy, we don't have the luxury of repetition. We want to get some kind of response. But, we can't expect someone to read your sales page or your copy five or six times.

Since we don't have that luxury, the best way to get that emotional bank account where we want it is by knowing your customer. You want to start with your customer. One of the biggest problems a lot of clients will have, and you may have this same problem when you are your own client, is they get so excited about the product that they forget that copy is not about the product, service, or info product. It's about the customer. You have to start with the customer:

Who is this person?

What's on their mind?

What's their life like?

These kinds of questions are the questions you need to ask.

Then, if you're solving a problem for them:

What is their problem?

What is their desire?

It is possible to see having a desire as a problem. Because if you want something and you don't have it, that's a problem.

What you are offering is a solution. Before you even start writing, figure out what your offer is. Don't worry about your headline. Don't worry about your bullets. Don't worry about your opening line. Think about your offer. What are you offering them? What are they going to get? What's the benefit? Get that clear in your mind.

There's an old saying that says mediocre copy and a good offer will out-pull great copy and a mediocre offer any day of the week. And it's true. Make a good offer and if your grammar is incorrect, if your spelling is bad, or even if you have orange type on a green background, it could still work.

So you start with your offer and then use the following formula:

Start with your headline. Now, I'm not saying you have to necessarily write it in this order. But, this is the order it will end up in.

Then, add an opening sentence that deepens the emotional

direction that the headline sets you off in. If the headline is a threat or a warning about a problem, you want to go into Negative Optism. We'll talk about Negative Optism later in this book.

If the headline is a promise of a promised land, a promise of something better, of something good, then you may be able to go ahead with a description of how good it's going to be once they take you up on your offer.

Then, unless the sales letter is to your list, unless it's to people who know you, love you, and trust you, then you want to put your credentials in. Credentials need to be relevant. If you are a refrigerator repairman and you went to MIT... or you are a member of MENSA... or you are one of the few people who knows how to dance a jig backwards doing acrobatic backflips... and if you were in fact in the semi-finals for the Olympics — nobody cares. Your client wants to know if you can repair his refrigerator, and if the Refrigeration Certification Counsel or the National Association of Refrigeration Repair has given you their highest quality award.

Credentials need to be relevant — not to you, but to your customer. Credentials really are what you have done or what people have said about you that have to do with what you're going to do for the customer. They are concerned about themselves. Their question is always going to be, "What's in it for me?"

Then you want to get into your offer. Your offer should not just what you're selling. It should be the benefit of it. The uniqueness of it. The bonuses. Any specific terms.

Then bullets. Once you get people excited about your offer, all of a sudden the mind finally kicks in. The mind has sort of been skiing, skating, or sledding until it comes time to make a decision, All of a sudden it's reality. They are thinking:

> Well, what's in it?
>
> What's it going to do for me?
>
> What are the details? What's it made out of?
>
> How long is it going to take?
>
> How long is it going to last?

Bullets are where you can really cover these things and answer those questions that are likely to be on your prospect's mind.

When someone gets to the point where they are about ready to buy, procrastination will kick in. They will try to think of every reason in the world not to buy.

What you need to do at this point is convince them that they have no other choice. There is nowhere else they can go. Either they take this offer or they lose out. They don't get what they were looking for. The problem that they were worried about will get worse. They are not going to get what they wanted. They need to see that this is the single best choice for them.

Then, you'll get into price. By the time people know that they can't really get it anywhere else, the price is pretty irrelevant. They'll spend their last dime if they have to.

Think of a family member that you really care about. If they were ill, you would spend your last dime.

Think of something you really want more than anything and you've spent your whole life wanting. How far you would go to get it?

You want to get them in that frame of mind. Price belongs in the copy after you have built up their desire and reasons to buy. It goes after you have gotten rid of their reasons not to buy.

Then you offer your guarantee so they feel safe buying.

You could use some sort of limitation to take it away. It could be a drop in price. It could be a limited quantity.

The signature, and a P.S. goes after that.

So, the parts that make up a successful letter are:

1. Headline
2. Open – Promise or Negative Optism (See Chapter 9)
3. Credentials
4. Offer
5. Bullets
6. Choice of one
7. Price
8. Guarantee
9. Takeaway
10. Signature
11. P.S.

We can build upon this framework to take your copywriting to new levels.

3

NOT WHAT YOU SAY, BUT HOW YOU SAY IT

The "C Factor" is conversation. Copywriting is a conversation with your reader. Or, if you're writing for audio or podcasting, it is a conversation with your listener. If you're creating video, it's a conversation with your viewer.

I had a client once who lived in a big town in the South. At one time, he lived on a street where there were lots of cars driving by. George and his little daughter Jeanine would often play on the front lawn. I asked him if she ever ran out into the street when she was playing (She was 2-3 years old at the time.)

He said, "Yes."

I asked him if Jeanine ever ran out into the street when a car was coming.

George said, "Yeah, there were times."

So I said to him, "I want you to take yourself back in time and remember when that occurred. What did you do? Did you stand on the front porch very calmly and say, "Jeanine I'd like to tell you about Newton's discoveries about physics. A body in motion tends to stay in motion, whereas a body at rest tends to stay at rest. And also, when a larger body in motion comes across a smaller body in motion, there tends to be displacement of mass?"

George agreed that's not what he would have said.

He said, "The first thing I would do is yell, 'STOP'!" Then he said, "Then I would go out into the street and I would take her by the hand, and I'd bring her back to the house."

I then asked him if he would have explained to her why she shouldn't run out in the street without looking both ways.

He agreed. He said, "Yeah, I would do that."

This is very much how it is when you are talking to your prospects. You want to do the same thing with your copy even though your prospect is not a little girl playing out on the front lawn. The same principles apply.

You want to say something that will make them stop. Stop where they are going as they are surfing the Web. Stop reading through their email. Stop reading through the newspaper. Or even stop perusing email headlines deciding what to delete.

You want to make them stop. Then, you want to grab them by the hand and lead them into your house. In this case, your house is the rest of your sales copy. You want to explain to them gently why they should have stopped in the first place. You want to tell them why what you have to offer is a benefit to them. You want to explain how it will enhance their lives or protect them, or whatever it will do. You also want to explain the consequences of getting your product and the consequences of not getting your product. You want to do this in a way where your copy accomplishes its purpose.

Now, if this seems overly simplistic to you, I understand. However, writing effective copy requires you to look at life at the ground level, in very simple terms. Copy needs to be like a very basic direct conversation with short words, short sentences, and no big concepts or vague abstractions.

Sometimes, the question or concern comes up, "Well, I don't want to sound like a simpleton." Or, "I don't want to talk down to my customers. My product is not simplistic. My service is not simplistic." Or, "Our business is not simplistic." So, how do we do all of these things?

Copy, as I define it, is a sales presentation in print.

If you think about that, I think you will realize that when you are giving a live sales presentation, most of the time the language is pretty simple. It's conversational and direct. It may not be colloquial or ungrammatical, but it is a little more relaxed than the formal written language that we were all taught to write in.

Copywriting is not the written language; it's the spoken language. In a way, it's a different language. It uses the same words. It looks like the same words. Conditioning, practice, and habit are very important. When they told me in school not to end a sentence with a preposition, that was just the beginning of a long conditioning process to teach you to write in a way that was not effective in selling. Why would they do that? Well, I don't know, but they did.

There are a number of things to know about conversation that are very important. The first thing is to learn to listen in a new way.

I took a screenwriting class once where we were learning to write dialogue. We were told to eavesdrop — to go to public places and listen to the exact words people were saying. Then, just write it up in movie dialogue format. It was a very powerful exercise.

Listening to people can be very useful for writing copy. Especially, if you listen to people fight, whine, or complain. You want your copy to be positive. But, it's those language structures that people use when they are letting their hair down, when they are not on guard, that add power to your copy.

Another shorthand way is to get the *National Enquirer*. A lot of copywriting teachers talk about this. One of the things I think that I can bring to the party that is new is that the *National Enquirer* is written in a way that is very much like a conversation. It's like hot gossip between two people whispering in loud, hot whispers.

That is a lot like the way you want your copy to be. You want your copy to be like you're telling a friend about a secret that's really exciting. So, first of all, you need to learn to recognize it. Secondly, start to write that way in your copy.

If you were a literary writer or a professor of English, you could find so many things wrong with The *National Enquirer*, including the fact that the language is trite and cliché-ridden. And that is my point. Because, that is how people talk. Most people talk in a trite and cliché-ridden way. That is why they are called clichés because many people use them lots of the time.

People don't come spinning out with Shakespearean eloquence. It's just not the way we talk as human beings. So, to see it written down is rare, especially written down in a very clear, concise, readable way. You can get that from the *Enquirer*. That is the first thing I suggest.

Now, can you take what you learn in the *Enquirer* and use it as a cookie-cutter template for your own copy?

Almost assuredly not — unless you're selling to the *Enquirer* crowd and it's a high-drama, very personal type of consumer product.

But you can take the techniques, principles and turns of phrase, and adapt them to your situation and circumstances.

As an additional bonus, you can almost get a platinum education in headline writing with the *Enquirer*.

Writing conversationally, with emotion, is hard for a lot of people.

I have a private coaching client who is a psychotherapist. He is doing very well with copywriting. We were working on some bullets. His profession has trained him to squeeze every ounce of emotion and bias out of his language that he can when he writes professional reports. Well, that's great for his professional reports. It's not so great for his copy.

So, we started rewriting some things. He wasn't really getting it. And I said to him, "Do you ever do couples counseling?" He said he did. I said, "Well, you know when couples aren't getting along, they are saying all the wrong things to each other. They say things like, 'You always do this' and 'You never do this,' — all the things that don't work in relationships? Those things work really great in copy."

It was like a light bulb went on at the other end of the phone several thousand miles away. He really got it. Because that is the emotion-laden language, not of the thinking mind, but of the habitual mind.

If you were to say, "The one thing you must always do before you write copy..." Must you always do it? Must you do it?

You could also say, "The one thing you should probably do most of the time before you write copy..." and that would maybe be just as accurate or even more accurate. But, it doesn't have the emotional impact the previous sentence has.

When it comes to copywriting, and the language used for copywriting, it's the same language, but it's not really the same language. I have a theory, and I have absolutely no scientific proof of this theory. Copywriting is the language of the right brain. The right brain — the part of your brain that's creative and deals with music, rhythm, pictures, and connects with the unconscious mind — that part of the brain does have a verbal vocabulary.

They found when portions of human brains have been severed, people are actually able to pronounce, use, and understand a very limited number of words. The severed brain has about the vocabulary of a ten-year-old or a fifth grader. Most copy that works is at about that level. I think when you're writing copy, even though it looks like normal language, it's really a subset of language. It is "right brain" language.

One of the great things about copy is it lets you take a successful sales pitch that you deliver in spoken form, to one prospect at a time, and multiply it.

Some simple math: If you have a winning formula with your spoken words, and you get a 1% response, and you put it in writing in front of 100,000 people:

That's 1% x 100,000, or 1,000 responses.

That saves you from having to make a whole lot of sales calls.

The problem comes in when you start out with a written sales pitch that would never work in a personal, spoken, one-on-one situation. That's like trying to to multiply zeros. No matter how many people you put those words in front of — you still get no response at all.

When you learn to write in a conversational way — a way that would work with a prospect in person — your results will improve. Learning to write conversationally is a skill that takes time, but is well worth the effort. The more your copy sounds like a real conversation, the more engaging it will be.

4

THE MOST IMPORTANT PART OF COPYWRITING

What do you need to know before you start writing copy?

As specifically as possible, before anything else, you need to know who your customer is and what market your customers make up. A lot of people say, "Well, my customers are everybody." Unless you are General Motors, Nabisco or Microsoft, you don't have the resources and the long timeline you would need to have your market be "everybody."

You need to have a very specific market. You want to narrowly define your market as closely as possible. For example: if you are doing a book on dogs, it would probably be better to target people who are interested in Australian Shepherds, rather than people who are interested in all dogs.

There are a number of things you want to know about your customers:

- How are these people in reality?
- What questions do they have?
- How do they feel?
- What is their lifestyle like?
- What keeps them awake at night?

The more you know your customer and your market, the better you will be able to write copy. Truth be told, you want to be able to feel like them to the point where figuratively you become them. You want to step into their shoes or even drop into their skin in your imagination. You want to see the world through their eyes, not yours.

Then you need to know about your product.

What's obvious to you is not obvious to them, unless they're already familiar with your product. You have to tell them what it's going to do for them. To do this, you may have to sit down and make a list again starting with the very obvious: Why would they want this? Why would they want this instead of a competitor's? Why is getting your product better than doing nothing?

When people in this market see it, what surprises them about your product? What do they say to you? Find ways to work that in, because remember, there's a learning curve with every product and if you're the one who has created it, well even if you're the one who is selling it, you're a lot more familiar with it than the person who is reading your sales copy. So you want to step back in time a little bit to where you were before you knew about this product or before you created it. You want to go back through the process of learning and discovering with your customers in your sales copy.

The third thing you need to know, and this is vitally important, is how to talk to your market in their own language. I use the example of a doctor I have an as a client who is selling unusual health supplements. The thing about doctors is, they talk in a different language. They went to medical school as many people have in many other professions. And the example I like to use is if a doctor has come up with a new cure for an upset stomach, the last thing he wants to do in his sales copy is talk about dyspepsia, which is the technical term doctors' use for an upset stomach.

Which words would work better?

"Upset stomach."

This may be pretty obvious to you. But, you'll probably find that you're using some words that are from your own area or from your own frame of reference. While it's not putting your market off, it is getting them out of the flow of desire while they are reading your copy and into "figuring it-out-mode."

When somebody goes into "figuring-it-out" mode, you lose momentum, and you reduce the number of sales.

5

EIGHTY PERCENT OF THE JOB

These are three things that are going to change your copy for the better. The first thing is a killer headline. There's nothing better than a killer headline to improve your response and make your copy work. The second thing is killer bullets. Bullets are bullet points, and we'll talk about that. The third thing is a killer offer.

Headlines are so important and make a huge difference in your copy. I have dedicated several podcast episodes discussing headlines in more depth at *The Copywriter's Podcast* (www.copywriterspodcast.com).

In order to write a killer headline, you have to understand a little bit about human psychology. There are seven main reasons people buy. These reasons you really need to keep top of mind. They are:

1. Make money
2. Save money

3. Save time
4. Save effort
5. Improve health
6. Increase pleasure
7. Eliminate pain

The first one is to make money. Not everyone buys to make money. Some people believe they can't make money. Their mission is to save money and to spend less.

In a business-to-business sale, making money is going to be hard for someone who's not at a top level in sales or the management of a company. But, to make money is important for an entrepreneur, a business opportunity seeker, a business owner, and a senior manager, as well as to save money.

Now, if you can show someone they can make money and save money, that's even better.

To save time is another reason. No one has enough time these days. So, if you can show people how to save time, that's great.

The next is to save effort. I have news for you — most people, given the opportunity are lazy.

Next is to improve health. People will spend a lot of money to improve health. Now, most of the time they will wait until an emergency. There are relatively few people, but it is getting more and more, who will spend money proactively and preventively to improve health.

Number six is increase pleasure. If you go to the casinos, in some of the more fancy places in Las Vegas, you will find people vending that at several hundred dollars a pop. They are usually of the female variety and they have very nice clothing. But, there are all kinds of other pleasure enhancing types of reasons people will spend money.

The last is to eliminate pain.

There are more reasons, but if you understand these seven, that will help you very much with what we're about to cover.

You may have read or heard someone say you should write 100 headlines using your swipe file. If you are unfamiliar with a swipe file, it's a collection of previous ads that have worked.

My problem with telling you to do that is that it would be like saying to you, "Would you please stand up and face the correct direction?" What is the correct direction? There are 360 possibilities at least. I think swipe files work great once you have an experience base. But, I think there is a training wheels aspect that you need to go through first in order to get that experience.

The solution to quickly writing effective headlines even when you don't have extensive experience is Copywriting Templates™. I've included many of the headlines that are included in my Copywriting Templates included with High Speed Copywriting home study course (www.highspeedcopywriting.com). I selected these particular templates because they have maximum, universal applicability. In English, that means anyone can use them for just about anything.

In other words, you start with the proven basics and you master those. My friend Patricia Fripp, who is a masterful speaker started out as a hairdresser. She became a masterful hairdresser.

She says you have to master style in order to abandon it. The same principle applies with copywriting.

You can use the following headline types to quickly write an effective headline.

Headline Type #1: "Who else wants to..."

Here's the proven headline: Who else wants to look like a movie star? That was for a beauty product from the 30's or 40's. There was another one when women measured their worth and status by how white their laundry was. It was, "Who else wants a whiter wash?" Both of those worked really well.

So, here is the template: "Who else wants..." This headline is very effective when your prospect has a desire or goal, and your naming it easily incites the awareness of it.

One thing to understand is that "wants" is not what your product does. It's what your customer wants. They don't want your product or process. They don't want the steps they go through. They want the end result, the big payoff, the big enchilada. That's what they want. They don't want to put some dye into their hair that's going to burn like hell on the scalp. They want to have hair that looks beautiful.

Do you see the difference? So, here are a couple of examples of using this:

> Who else wants a six-figure residual income?
>
> Who else wants to get luxury products at Wal-Mart prices?

Are you starting to see the make money, save money, and how that works?

> Who else wants the sexual pleasure you've only dreamed about?

That one is sort of sneaky because if you've dreamed about it, you want it. If they are stimulation or pleasure junkies, they'll go for that.

This headline may look a little weird to you when you're not the target market for this headline. "Who Else Wants To Look Like A Movie Star?" might sound a little ridiculous.

"Who Else Wants to be Able to Think Like a Copywriter Without Having to Go Through All of the Strife, and Struggle?" All of a sudden, it doesn't seem ridiculous anymore because you're engaged.

Headline Type #2: "Give Me... And I'll..."

Here is another headline template. "Give me 5 days, and I'll give you the secret of learning any subject."

This headline can be used when you can deliver results much more quickly than people are accustomed to thinking it takes to deliver the results.

"Give me 5 days," or give me a surprisingly short amount of time, "and I will give you" an end result your prospect dearly wants. Give me a certain amount of time and I'll give you a certain result.

By the way, I know that's a learning example, but it doesn't have to be a learning example. If you could tune up a car in 15 minutes, you could say, "Give me 15 minutes and I'll tune up your car perfectly." You could use it for a lot of different things.

This template works especially well if speed is part of your unique competitive advantage. It doesn't mean you have to do everything fast. But, if there is something you can do faster than people generally expect, that's a great advantage to spotlight or highlight in the headline.

Headline Type #3: "Do You Recognize The 7 Early Warning Signs Of..."

"Do you recognize the seven early warning signs of high blood pressure?"

This is the type of headline that people with high blood pressure or who have family members with high blood pressure will sit up and take notice of. That is the power of targeting a specific audience. Some won't care or take any notice, but others will zoom in on it.

Examples of "Do you recognize the seven early warning signs of..."

> Do you recognize the seven early warning signs of entrepreneurial meltdown?
>
> Do you recognize the seven early warning signs that your bank will freeze your merchant account?

This one is about fears, and about something someone doesn't want to happen. This is about avoiding pain.

Headline Type #4: "Get Rid of (Problem) Once And For All"

This headline is best used when your prospects have a problem they are well aware of and will quickly recognize and acknowledge it just by your naming the problem.

By the way, you need to be able to solve the problem in order to use this headline, or your ad's not going to be believed. And, remember, that's the most important thing.

Some examples of how this can be used are:

> Get Rid Of Your Retirement Worries Once And For All
>
> Get Rid Of That Rumpled Look Once And For All
>
> Get Rid Of that Feeling of Overwhelm Once And For All
>
> Get Rid Of Those Sleepless Nights Once And For All

Headline Type #5: "Thousands Now..."

This is number four: "Thousands Now Play Who Never Thought They Could."

This was an ad for pianos and learning how to play the piano with a correspondence course.

Of course, a lot of people think: "I'm tone deaf. I can't play a note; I can't sing a note."

The headline said, "Thousands Now Play Who Never Thought They Could."

The template here is:

> Thousands Now _______(do something) Who Never Thought They Could

Let me give you a few examples of how to use it:

> Thousands Now Kick Box Who Never Thought They Could
>
> Thousands Now Fly Planes Who Never Thought They Could
>
> Thousands Now Drive Austin Cars Who Never Thought They Could
>
> Thousands Now Take Beautiful Pictures Who Never Thought They Could

This headline can be used when you have a product or service that provide a result people desperately want, but they really don't think they could ever achieve it. To effectively use this, you need to be able to prove in your copy that others have used your product or service to achieve this result.

Headline Type #6: "Build A... You Can Be Proud Of"

"Build a Body You Can Be Proud Of."

Obviously, this was a bodybuilding ad.

People are much more emotional about things than they let on. I don't just mean the things they are very emotional about – I mean everything.

A lot of people are secretly dissatisfied with just about every aspect of their lives.

If you have a product, a service, or an information product that can help them improve their life in any way, then you're in a very good position to use this headline and to build your whole sales message off of it.

For example, a landscaping service could say, "Have a Yard That You Can be Proud Of." Well, if you don't have a yard, or if you're already proud of your yard, you might laugh at that. But, if your yard looks like the Mojave Desert, and everyone else's looks like a lush tropical jungle, that might really reach out to you.

So, the key thing here is you really need to get to know your customers better than you ever have before, and understand what's on their minds. You need to know:

- What's bothering them?
- What are their secret hopes?
- What are their dreams?
- What are the things they complain about to their family and friends when they let their hair down?

And you start to work that into your copy.

If somebody starts to say things about their lawn that they're ashamed about, such as "The crabgrass has taken over," and you know what those specific things are, you could use that as part of the copy in your ad.

Headline Type #7: "See How Easily..."

The original headline was, "See How Easily You Can Learn to Dance This New Way."

The template is: "See How Easily You Can ________ This New Way"

A couple different ways this could be used are:

See How Easily You Can Get Beautiful Portraits Made

See How Easily You Can Own a Persian Rug

See How Easily You Can Try Acupuncture

See How Easily You Can Have a Great Website

See How Easily You Can Get Publicity For Your Business

See How Easily You Can Get More Done This Way

Headline Type #8: "Do You Make These Mistakes..."

"Do You Make These Mistakes in English?"

This headline helps people avoid costly mistakes that others often make — where you can demonstrate, in your copy, how the mistakes people typically make are indeed costly.

Some examples of how it could be used include:

Do You Make These Computer Mistakes?

Are You Making Any of These Financial Mistakes?

Do You Make These Web Marketing Mistakes?

Do You Make These Management Mistakes?

Headline Type #9: "What's New In..."

This one is going to seem pretty silly now, but at the time, it was good.

"What's New in Summer Sandwiches?"

Does anyone care about summer sandwiches any more? Maybe you do, I don't know.

Here is how you adapt this headline for your business:

"What's New in __________..." something that your customer buys from you, is familiar with, and is interested in.

People are very focused on their interests. So, if you had a day care center, you might send out to all of your clients: "What's New in Day Care?"

A tour bus company could send out to tour directors or association executives: "What's New in Group Tours?"

A home entertainment company might send out to audio/video buffs: "What's New in High Definition TV?"

A bike shop might send out: "What's New in Mountain Bikes?" Or, they could put it on the website.

Don't use this headline if you don't have anything that's really new and different. Don't stretch on this one. Don't try to come up with something new and different when it's not. Only use this headline when you have something that is truly new and different and would be important to your readers.

Headline Type #10: "The Lazy..."

If you are older like me, you might remember a very interesting guy named Joe Karbo from the 70's or 80's. He used to run full-page ads in newspapers with the headline, "The Lazy Man's Way to Riches." It was a long ad with lots of stories in it. He was telling about how he used mail-order and information products to become very, very rich.

Of course, he was selling an information product by mail order to get even richer. He came up with a great headline: "The Lazy Man's Way to Riches."

A lot of people are not lazy, but they have so many things to do that they feel like they're lazy.

They will respond to an appeal that says, "The Lazy Man's Way."

Here is one for a headhunter: "The Lazy Executive's Way to Get a Great New Job." See, it doesn't matter whether a person is really lazy or not.

They will read this because here is what goes on in their mind: "I actually work pretty hard. But, if I were a lazy person, I wouldn't want to do very much work to get a new job. Frankly, I'm too busy with this, that, and the other thing. I would like someone else to do it for me. So, I think I'll read the rest of this ad."

How about for a limo service, or a car service: "The Lazy Person's Way to Get Around Town."

For self storage: "The Lazy Person's Way to Deal With Too Much Stuff'."

I hope you're getting some ideas here.

These headline templates don't only work for headlines. They will also work for subheads.

You could say, "What We've Really Discovered is the Lazy Person's Way to Write Copy."

6

HOW ONE SENTENCE CAN CLOSE THE SALE FOR YOU

What are bullets? A lot of people don't really understand bullets and bullet points. In terms of what they are technically, the little dots are bullets and the words after them are the bullet points.

But from a copywriting point of view, remember that we're trying to move someone from resistance into action. It's almost as though there is a balance scale filled with BB's. The bullet points are like BB's that move the desire to take action high enough, so there is no resistance. Bullet points are little things, any one of which could take a person over the edge and could shift the balance scale.

A bullet is a short phrase — sometimes as long as 2 or 3 lines. In a very concentrated and power-packed dynamic way, it sums up what is really powerful or exciting, usually about one aspect about what you're writing your copy about.

A lot of people don't understand what a bullet is supposed to do, or how it's supposed to do that. A bullet point is not a summary. It is not a condensation. A bullet doesn't just lie on the floor in a pile of goo. A bullet is something in action.

For instance, take a table fan on an extremely hot day. The blade of the fan is a feature of the fan. It isn't a bullet. A bullet is the breeze that is created by the fan blade. It is what makes the person feel comfortable.

If you ever get stuck on bullets, think of your prospect as someone who is hot and sweaty and your product or your service is the fan that's going to cool them off and make them feel comfortable again. You have to get them to imagine that comforting, soft breeze that's calming them down. A bullet is your product in motion.

If you were selling a weight loss product, you would not want to use "Powerful Weight Loss Plan" as one of your bullets. That's a summary; that doesn't work.

It doesn't work because it satisfies and you don't want to satisfy the prospect.

What do you want to do? You want to provoke them. You want them to read the next sentence. You want to create curiosity, desire, anxiety, and excitement. You don't want to create that static state of satisfaction.

If your bullet doesn't get someone excited or get someone craving some of the benefit that your product is going to provide — whether your product is providing relief from anxiety, relief from pain, money, hope, opportunity, or whatever your product is providing — the bullet needs to get them into the experience by arousing their emotions.

You don't want them to say, "Now I understand what it is. I don't have to worry about getting it because I understand what it is." What you want them to understand is why they want to buy it. Why they want to take action. Creating satisfaction does not accomplish this goal. Intrigue, curiosity, and desire make the person want to know more or want to do something. The person wants to take the action you want them to take.

This is not a bullet for a weight loss product: "When you're trying to lose weight, you should never eat two ice cream sized scoops of Crisco covered with a generous serving of maple syrup. In this book, you'll learn why."

This is a bullet: "A double whammy dessert that's a recipe for diabetes and high cholesterol. You may have had this after Sunday dinner, but after you learn what it is, you'll never even think of eating this again."

What's the difference? I'm talking about the same thing. People eat foods that are actually that bad. In the first case, I'm describing it. Now you know what not to eat, so where does that leave you? "I understand something. I learned something. That's great."

With the second bullet point, you want them to say, "What's he talking about? Is he talking about my favorite dessert? Am I going to get diabetes from my favorite dessert? Am I going to get high cholesterol? I'm going to have a heart attack just because of my favorite dessert?"

Bullets are important when you are writing copy because, with the type of sales copy I'm discussing here, people cannot see your product. They can't feel it or hold it. They can't try it out. They can't take it home. Bullets are dynamic. They are your product in action.

You can tell if bullets are good by how people react. A bullet needs to be more than just merely interesting. Bullets need to reach out and grab someone by the emotions to the point where that person says, "How can I get that?" or "How do they do that?" or "What is that?" or "What are they talking about?"

Bullet Type #1: "Number Bullet"

The first kind of bullet is called a Number Bullet because it has a number in it.

This type of bullet can be used when you want to make what you are selling more tangible and concrete.

Here are some examples of Number Bullets:

Five ways to ___________

Seven steps to __________

Thirteen things you should know about ________

Eleven time saving __________

Nine insider techniques that will _________

147 resources for __________

These types of bullets create curiosity, desire and other emotions that will keep a person moving forward.

The numbers used here are just examples and should be changed to the specific number directly related to your product. If you do have odd numbers, they seem to work better. I don't know why they do, but somehow they do.

An example of this type of bullet being used is:

> Five simple steps that subtract two or more hours out of every copywriting assignment

I can guarantee this is a bullet that would appeal to anyone who writes copy as part of his or her work, or for a living. One of the problems with copy is that it takes a long time. That's one of the reasons I created my Copywriting Templates™, included with the membership website www.fasteffectivecopy.com with my partner Brian McLeod, and the High Speed Copywriting Seminar and DVD product — to help people save time when they write copy.

Compare these two bullets:

> I'll show you a way to subtract two or more hours out of every copywriting assignment.

Versus

> Five simple steps that subtract two or more hours out of every copywriting assignment.

In both cases, you're probably going to believe me because you've already seen how I'm able to do this, and how you've been able to save time just with what you have seen from the templates so far. But, notice the "Five simple steps..." See how it makes it more tangible?

That is what a good bullet accomplishes.

Bullet Type #2: The Secrets Bullet

Secrets of ___________

The secret to ___________

A secret method for ___________

The dirty little secret that ___________ don't want you to know

The secret reason that ___________

This bullet type can be used when you have a benefit in your product that people outside of your business don't know about that will deliver an important benefit.

I got one of those Internet jokes that said, "A mother said to her little boy when she was trying to teach him how to put on a coat, 'The secret is to put the zipper part into the left-hand part.' The little boy said, 'Why does it have to be a secret?'" I sent that to my mother and said, "Did this ever happen when I was little?" She said, "No, because I didn't talk to you that way." I'm glad I didn't learn copywriting from my mother.

Here are some examples:

Secrets of high profile sales on eBay.

Secrets of managing your insurance agency more profitably.

Secrets of golfers with Zen-like calm.

The secret reason that women buy more shoes than they wear.

Those are intriguing, right?

Bullet Type #3: "Tremendous Benefit Bullets"

The third one takes a little more understanding, but it's not that hard. This is the "Tremendous Benefit Bullet." This is like the balance where you use just a little bit of force to get a lot of outcome. For example, "a little bit goes a long way," or "Zippity do – a little dab will do ya."

Here are some examples:

Here's one: "A tiny little __________ that __________.

Here's another one: "In less than five minutes, you can ____________.

A little known ____________that will ____________.

An easy ____________ to ____________.

How an ordinary __________ that costs less than _________ can __________.

Bullet Type #4: "A Tiny Little... That Will..."

"A tiny little…that will…"

With this bullet, something that is perceived as small is used to achieve an outcome that your customer wants.

Some examples of how these can be used:

> A tiny little phrase that will double your sales.
>
> In less than five minutes, you can write a headline that will double your response.
>
> A little known South American herb that will turn her into a volcano of roaring passion.

This is about a tiny little thing that will have a huge outcome. With this type of bullet, you want to take a small piece, action, time segment, or effect involved with using your product or service that delivers the greatest result and highlight it.

Bullet Type #5: "In less than five minutes, you can..."

Here's another one: "In less than five minutes, you can ____________."

Let's say that you were selling a language course for people traveling to other countries.

What is one of the biggest problems people have? They always feel like they are getting charged a premium because they have "sucker" written all over their foreheads.

> In less than five minutes, you'll stop getting tourist prices when you are shopping on your vacation, and they'll start offering you the 'natives only' real bargains.

See, five minutes turns into much better prices for your souvenirs, curios, and knickknacks from your vacation.

Bullet Type #6: "A little known... that will..."

Here's another one: "A little known __________ that will __________."

> A little known move less than 1% of all martial artists know that a 105-pound woman can easily use to deck a 300-pound man in no time flat.

I think this exists as an archetype deep in our minds. There are movies, pictures, and dramas playing out in our minds all the time. We are looking for them in stories people tell. So, if you have something you can represent legitimately this way — poetically, but legitimately — then you should. It will satisfy people whether or not they buy it. It will give them something that they need; a kind of imagination stimulation they are craving.

Bullet Type #7: "Exclusive Quality Bullet"

The next kind of bullet is called an "Exclusive Quality Bullet."

Now, you may or may not be able to use this yourself because it depends on the kind of product that you're offering. Every product is unique, but when I'm talking about exclusive, I'm really talking almost about the snob factor here. Not everyone is in that kind of carriage trade, or fancy luxury market. But, if you have a number of different products, and one of them is your high end product, your flagship product, your flagship service, or your flagship information product, then this would be good.

So, here are the bullets.

One of them is "The only __________."

These are like titles. They're like tags. They don't have to be sentences. A piano store could use this bullet like this:

> The only store in town that carries the same piano that the Philharmonic insists on.

Do you see the exclusivity there? The professional orchestra has a piano they insist on, and we're the only store in town. So, there's some exclusivity there. Some of this is about writing. Some of this is about how you examine your products, your customers, and the marketplace to figure out where you have your business strategic advantages and your strategic marketing advantages.

Here's another one: "This unique, patented formula…"

> This unique, patented formula reduces wear and tear while actually improving engine life by up to 67%.

If you have a very high-end version of an additive and it's expensive, but it has some great test results, (and it might not have anything to do with high-end automotive supplies) this is a good example

Here's your ultimate high-end appeal:

> Why people in Beverly Hills and Geneva pay ______.
>
> Why people in Beverly Hills and Geneva pay up to 200% of suggested list price for our watches.

Now, that might be more of a subhead or a headline.

Let's say you were a jeweler, and you were putting on a seminar for other jewelers. They are having trouble maintaining their margins, and you're getting 100% over list. That would be a pretty good bullet.

"Our purchasing inspectors reject nine out of ten __________."

> Our purchasing inspectors reject nine out of ten diamonds, even though many have 'no flaws' according to the standards of our competitors.

That just cuts the legs out from under your competitors because it basically says their level of perfection isn't good enough for us.

I didn't say this is all nice; it's not. Sometimes, it's a machete fight out there. But, depending on what kind of competitive situation you're in, it's good to know these things.

Here's an interesting one.

Instead of saying, "We're the best" or "We're the top of the heap," you can use this, and it can be a bullet point. "People call us the best because" and then you come up with your reason. Suddenly, it's not you saying you're the best; it's other people saying you're the best. And, it's not only that, but you're giving them a reason, so it makes it a lot more believable.

Here's an example:

"People call this raincoat 'the best' because every top executive we know wears one."

Well, if you're a top executive in town and you find out about that, maybe you better wear one. You can use pressure and social proof. It is not necessarily the gentlest, kindest way to do things, but it works.

You will use this kind of bullet when you have something that's not available everywhere, or maybe hardly anywhere. People want what they can't have.

So, highlighting the exclusivity increases the attractiveness of your offer.

Bullet Type #8: "How To Bullet"

The next bullet group is the "How To Bullet."

"How To Bullets" do not literally use the words "how to." It's a very important distinction I want to make here. Understand the difference between process and result.

Very often, when you are the entrepreneur, the founder, the creator, the author, the manager, the marketing manager, or the copywriter, you're going to be looking inward toward the business rather than looking at the business from the outside in the way a customer does.

Here's the best example I like to give; it's my Dale Carnegie example. Dale Carnegie wrote a best selling book, which I highly recommend – How to Win Friends and Influence People.

What if he had named the book How to Remember People's Birthdays and Curb Your Incessant Urge to Argue? Do you think it would have been named the business book of the 20th Century by British Airways? Do you think it would have sold 15 million copies? I don't think so.

I bring this up because two of the most important things I got from the book are: no one can ever win an argument; and, it's important to remember personal things about people like their birthdays. But, that's the process. That's the stuff. That's the content. That's not the result. The result was winning friends and influencing people if you do those kinds of things.

I think by now you can see how bullets are concentrated. They are actually like real bullets. I think of packing gunpowder into a shell. When somebody reads them, it fires off an emotional charge in them.

The words are very compacted — very few words. They are really very similar to headlines.

In some ways, they are interchangeable with headlines.

Remember, what you are trying to do is keep the person reading the next sentence with your copy. You want to keep moving away from doubt and towards desire, certainty, and willingness to try and buy what you're selling.

If you think of your product as a cube of cheese (even if you're not selling cheese, just for illustration) and you were to cut the cube of cheese up into tiny little cubes, each bullet would be one cube, one mini-cube. Customers that you're not even talking to, and you've never even met are going to have different reasons why they want to buy your product or service.

Bullets give you the opportunity to appeal to a lot of different people in a very short space.

So, if a bullet hits a bull's-eye with somebody, if it really rings their bells and strikes a chord and they feel like it is something they want, one line, one bullet, can take them over the edge.

But, another person may need to see a different aspect.

7

WHAT MAKES PROSPECTS DROOL

After you have your headline and bullets down, you need to have an offer. An offer is really the heart of copy. Your offer is what makes somebody realize that they want something that you are selling. An offer is not what you are selling. An offer is what a person can do with what you are selling, all of the components, the big picture of your product, service or information product.

Even better, an offer is the big picture of what you are selling will do for your prospect. It is not just what they can do with it; it is what it will do for them. People like to have things done for them in the real world when they buy your products. An offer includes the bonuses and the guarantee.

A product offer includes how the prospect will use your product. You talk about the problems the prospect has had in the past. You show how your prospect will no longer have this problem with your product.

You describe the product in action. This is very important: describe them using it and describe it working with all of its components, bonuses and guarantees. Show how the prospect's problem is gone and how their life is much better.

Last Sunday night, I went out to a Japanese restaurant after working pretty late. Maggie, the waitress, comes up to me. She knows me. I was going to order some Teriyaki or something.

She looked at me and said, "David, you look pretty hungry."

I said, "Yeah."

She said, "You need some sake." She gets me some sake. And then I order. She said, "Are you sure that's going to be enough? You look really hungry."

And then, as my food comes, she said, "You know, I'm really hungry. I haven't eaten." And by the time it was over, I'd probably ordered about twice as much food and twice as much sake as I had planned to.

Now, the reason I'm telling you this is she made an offer to me. Her offer was sort of indirect, but it was very much to the point. She had put me in touch, or for that matter, manufactured some needs that I had and then she had presented some opportunities for me to fill those needs — mainly to have more to eat and drink. That was a product offer that she made to me just in the course of everyday business.

What an Offer Is

An offer is not your product, service or information product.

An offer is a solution. It's a package. It's the way you present your product, service or information product.

You present it in such a way that people see the value. It seems tangible to them. They start salivating for it. They want it and they feel good after they've spent the money. I'm sure you'd like to learn how to do that. I'm going to give you exact cookbook recipes for how to put together really good offers.

Three Kinds of Offers

We're going to talk about three kinds of offers because there are basically three kinds of things that you can sell.

The first thing is a product. A product is something that is physical. It's tangible. You can hold it in your hand. You can see it. You can take a picture of it. That's what a product is.

Then, there's a service. A service is something you do for somebody. You know what these things are, but I'm defining them for the purpose of offers.

And finally, there is an information product. In the world that a lot of us live in, information products are sort of in a class by themselves. They are technically products, but because they are so highly priced and there is so much value built in, sometimes it is difficult for people to convey how much value there is in an information product offer.

Four Things You Should Know About Offers

Here are four things that you should know about offers.

The first thing, as I've said, is an offer is not just what you're selling. If you simply do the best job you can of describing objectively what it is you're selling, you haven't made an offer. If you do this, you're not going to make as many sales as you could if you put a good offer together.

The second thing you should know is an offer is what a person can do with what you're selling. The more you describe what a person can do in your sales copy, the better. Remember the old idea of the fan blade being a feature. The fan blowing a soft breeze across you on a hot summer day, that is a benefit because it's the fan in motion. The offer is the product in motion in its totality. Whereas bullets, which we talked about in the previous chapter, are one aspect of the product in motion.

The offer is the big picture of the product in motion.

The third thing you should know about an offer is it's even better if your offer tells what you're selling will do for the person. There's an old story running around in copywriting education. I believe Dan Kennedy came up with it first. Everyone tells this story. It's about a printer who made a mistake. Someone was selling a home study course on learning how to play the piano or some kind of musical instrument. Originally the headline was: "Put Music in Your life." Well, that's an offer right in the headline. Put music in your life. You can put music in your life.

One day, the printer screwed up and put an "s" after the "t" in "put," so it said: "Puts Music in Your Life." They got three times as many sales for the same circulation, the same number of clicks, and the same number of impressions.

The thinking behind that — the theory that people have come up with to explain that — which I believe to be true, is when the person doesn't have to do anything and when they envision having it done to them or for them, or without any effort on their part, then they will want it even more. So, "Puts Music in Your Life" does it for you. "Put Music in Your Life" implies some effort on your part.

When you can vividly get the prospect to visualize what your product, service, or information product will do for them, that's even better.

The fourth thing you need to know about offers is you can add bonuses. Bonuses are very interesting. Offering bonuses doesn't mean going around your shop or your warehouse or your library or your hard drive thinking, "Hmm, what else can I just throw in here to add bulk?"

Bonuses can be used strategically to drive more sales.

Psychology of Bonuses

There is a psychology of bonuses, which boils down to: the bonus springs out of the offer. In other words, the offer is going to offer to solve a problem or help someone meet a desire. Each bonus should extend that power or that aspect of the offer.

For instance, I'm going to give you a real simple example. If your product says: "Here's How To Attract Pennies Into Your Life," then a bonus could be, "Here's How To Attract Five-Dollar Bills Into Your Life." The second bonus could be, "Here's How To Attract Hundred Dollar Bills Into Your Life."

Each bonus is increasing the direction and power of the offer. Obviously, no one is going to believe this particular language, but it's a good illustration.

Speaking of money, you might want to know that pricing can be part of your offer. The way you set up your payment plan can be part of your offer. Not charging someone's credit card for two weeks or 30 days or not cashing their check can be part of your offer. Likewise, your guarantee can be part of your offer.

Remember, when people are reading your copy, they're not thinking, "Hmm, I wonder what the offer is?" They don't go over it with a mental checklist.

What's going on in their mind is, "Wow, what's it going to be like if I buy this?" "What's the upside?" "What's the downside?" "How can I get hurt?" "How can I avoid getting hurt?" "How am I going to benefit?"

All of these little things I'm talking about — the pricing, the guarantee, the bonuses, portraying your product or service through the offer, portraying it as what it can do for somebody — all of those things add to the positive feelings and desire they want. They take away from their fear, hesitancy, and anxiety.

There are other things that you can do. You can add side benefits. If you buy this, you'll also have access to this club or this website or these discounts. What you are doing is you are using your imagination to create a whole new situation for the person. A practical situation that is going to meet their needs and wants and solve a problem they have come to you to solve even better with every little piece of the offer.

Keys to Creating Great Offers

Let me give you the keys to creating great offers.

The first key to creating great offers is to understand that your prospect has some questions. If your offer answers these questions, then you'll have a much better chance of closing the sale. The first question is, "What do I have to do to get it?" Then, "How do I order it?" "What is it going to cost?"

The second question they have on their mind is, "How can I be sure that it will work and that I'm getting my money's worth?" That can be answered by your guarantee. Then they are wondering, "What else do I get?" That will be answered by your bonuses and your side benefits, your special terms, your payment, your pricing, any discounts, any incentives that you have for early ordering, any specials and so forth.

Offer Type #1: "Product Offer"

There are three kinds of offers. The first kind is the "Product Offer." The purpose of this offer is to maximize the perceived and real value of your product. Whatever product you're selling, people are going to assume that it is not worth as much money as it really is. They want to spend less money.

It is human nature. If you can show people how much it is going to help them, how much it is going to make their life better, how it is going to help them make money or save money, or save time or save effort, then they will start to see your offer is the best place to do it.

I'm going to give you an example. This is not a real example, but it is certainly an example that I would like to see. Like many people, I have a terrific amount of frustration dealing with DVD equipment. It doesn't seem easy to use to me.

I invented a DVD machine in my mind that has some special instruction aids or learning aids that really brings it to life. It does this well beyond just the typical manual that was translated from another language.

You can use this as an offer template for any product that you're selling, It's an easy way to add value. Just follow what this does.

Here's the example:

> You can do so many things that you want to do with your new DVD recorder-player that you probably won't know where to start.
>
> That's where our Easy Start System comes in.
>
> Of course, you'll want to watch DVDs. But you'll also want to record and create custom DVDs, and duplicate your favorite recordings so you can share with friends and family.
>
> With Easy Start, all you have to do is turn to the right page of the Easy Start handbook. It's coil bound, so it lies flat so you can look at the step-by-step illustrated instructions.
>
> Or just pop the DVD into the player and click on the short video that shows you exactly how to do what you want to do. There are fourteen great video segments and each one only takes three minutes to watch.
>
> Not only that, we have an illustrated, narrated, step-by-step

> tutorial on the Internet, so you can get exact instructions right from your computer.
>
> Finally, you'll have a DVD player-recorder and know exactly how to use it. And this one is as easy to use as anything you've ever seen.

Notice what I did. The bonuses I added were not like 20 recordable DVDs or a microphone to add narration. What I did was add information to the product, but not just any kind of information. The information I added was not like the history of DVDs or 120 jokes about DVDs. I added information that solves a problem that most of us have had.

If you do something like that, you can add $50 or $100 to the price tag and people will pay it. Not everybody, not the price shoppers, not the people who are trying to get it cheap, but the people who actually want to use it and want to enjoy it and don't want the headaches.

The purpose of this approach is to maximize perceived and real value of your product.

Here are the steps to creating this offer:

1. How the prospect will use your product.
2. Address the problem they may have had using this type of product in the past, or a problem they will probably imagine having using your product
3. Offer information in a convenient to use form that solves the problem for them.
4. Describe the information so they can easily visualize using it.

5. Confirm that they no longer will have the problem because of how you've made your product so much easier to use.

After all, how many people in this industry are really going out of their way to show you how to use their products so that it comes to life where it is simple, illustrated and written in a user-friendly manner? Not very many.

When you add information that's unique, then you're going to capture a piece of the market that people might not have gotten.

Offer Type #2: "Service Offer"

This is a "Service Offer." Many people sell services. One of the biggest problems many marketing consultants say they have is that most other people selling services just don't charge enough for their services. I would say part of the reason for that is market forces driving the prices down.

But much of the time, the reason people are not able to ask for and get the monetary value that is equivalent to what they are delivering is that they haven't been able to describe what they do in a way that conveys the value. That's what this kind of offer is all about.

I will give you a for instance because I'm actually thinking of doing a monthly copywriting coaching program. I wrote an offer for it:

> There's never been a more certain, more effective way of learning how to write great copy than the Master Copywriting

> Coaching program. You can tune into each session and watch on your computer as you listen on the phone or you can even listen directly from your computer.
>
> You'll learn from real examples that are working today and you'll get your own copy critiqued and proof-read right on the spot. Plus, you will also see how the copy of others can be improved.
>
> Plus, you get a private newsletter every month with detailed examples and insider insights to show you what some of the smartest marketers are doing with their copy to make money.
>
> Best of all, you'll get the confidence backed by your own increasingly successful results. You'll become proficient in the most valuable skill in business, which is copywriting.

In this offer, the first thing I did was I described the service and described the unique and valuable qualities of the service: "a more certain, effective way of learning quickly how to write great copy." Then I gave additional details about what makes the service so valuable: "you'll learn from real examples that are working today and you'll get your own copy critiqued and improved right on the spot and you'll see how the copy of others can be critiqued."

You add one or more bonuses that build on the core appeal that you're making in the first place: "plus, you'll get a private newsletter every month with detailed examples and insider insights to show you what some of the smartest marketers are doing with their copy to make big money."

You summarize by highlighting how the prospect's situation

will be better, ideally, how it will be better in the long haul, because they purchased this service: "best of all you'll get confidence backed by your own increasingly successful results. You will become proficient in the most valuable skill in business."

Here's the key. This is where a lot of people miss opportunities.

This is what I avoided doing and this is what I was successful in doing by not missing the opportunity. I created an offer for a service, but before I did that I thought about what the service is and does at its most basic level.

I looked for the unique qualities that set it apart and then I looked for the most inventive and least expensive things I could do to add to the core proposition — the basic service itself, the monthly coaching program — to make it seem as valuable as possible.

That's why I say copywriting is strategic thinking.

The writing isn't nearly as important as the thinking: getting into the customer's mind; understanding what they really want in the first place. And then thinking, "What can I do to make it more valuable, to deliver more of that same value in a way that costs me as little as possible and delivers as much real value to them as possible?", while also having them realize that it delivers real value.

The steps to creating an offer like this are:

1. Describe the unique and valuable qualities of the service.
2. Give key additional details about what makes the service so valuable.

3. Add one or more bonuses that build on the core appeal you're making in the first place.
4. Summarize and conclude by highlighting how the prospect's situation will be better — ideally, how it will be better for the long haul — because they purchase this service.

To create a great offer for a service, think first about what the service is and what it does at the most basic level.

Then, look for unique qualities that set it apart from everything else the customer is considering instead.

Finally, look at the most inventive and least expensive things you can add to the core proposition (the basic service itself) to make it seem as valuable as possible.

The smartest marketers figure out what their offer is first, before they write their headline, before they write their bullets, before they do anything else. Then they build their copy around the offer.

Remember at the beginning, I said that the offer is at the heart of copy? Well, that's what it means. That's how it plays out. Marketers figure out what their offer is first and build their copy around the offer.

What the offer is, I think as you can see, is a combination of features and benefits in action, in such a way that it connects emotionally with the prospect who is qualified, who is right, who is ready for this kind of solution.

8

HOLLYWOOD, MEET COPYWRITING

What is the single best way to reach into the reader's heart, soul, and mind? The answer: a story. When you're with a little kid and you open up your mouth to say, "Let me tell you a story," what happens? Their eyes dilate wide and they get glassy, and the child goes into a trance.

We know about all kinds of stories. Little children say, "Tell me a story." American author and mythologist Joseph Campbell talked about story. What we are going to talk about here is a lot more specific than that. We are going to talk about "sales stories." These are stories that you can actually use in your copy to increase your sales.

One thing I would like you to know is that you don't always need stories in your copy. If you have something that people already want and they are already familiar with you, all you really need is a headline, some bullets and a call to action. And that will work just fine.

But, there are times when there is sales resistance. And stories are really the best way to reduce or eliminate sales resistance.

I got something out of a 1937 book called *Tested Sentences That Sell*, by Elmer Wheeler. He said, "W.W. Powell, the Hoover Company, sold 92% of the people who had signs on their doors saying, 'No canvassers or beggars allowed.' When I asked him what his reasoning was, he told me that only people with weak sales resistance put up those signs after they had bought so much from front porch salesmen that they had secured the sign for sales protection."

That's worth thinking about. To me, that is a little more aggressive than I am suggesting that you be. But, understand that some people will buy almost anything. Some people will buy without a lot of resistance. But other people have resistance. There are three kinds of resistance they have that stories can really help you with.

The first is skepticism. People aren't likely to believe you.

The second one is unfamiliarity. People not knowing who you are or knowing you at all exemplify that. They could also be unfamiliar with your product or your service and whether or not they need it.

And, the third thing is the price. When you are selling a high-priced product, no matter how good you are, there is going to be some sales resistance. If you have sold high-priced products in person or over the Internet, you have probably had that experience.

The Key Ingredient of Stories: Motion

So let's talk about stories, not in the global sense, not in the mythical sense, but just in a very functional, basic sense.

How will you know something is a story? I am going to give you some examples.

First of all, this is not a story:

A man was standing in front of a house.

Why is it not a story? Because there is no action.

Stories don't have to be long. This statement is only a little longer than the previous one. But this time, it is a story:

A man was moving into his new house. A bird flew by. It reminded him of a lost love, and tears welled up in his eyes.

Why is that a story? Because there is action. Something is happening. Somebody is moving. That is actually a story.

Yet, it's not much longer than the original which was not a story.

The Power of Stories

Let's talk about stories and why they are so powerful. *Stories are very powerful because stories bypass the typical thinking we have that puts up resistance, which is known as critical thinking.*

I like to say that people can argue with an opinion. They can argue with an assertion. They can argue with a claim. But, it's pretty hard to argue with a story. They might not believe the story. But, they are not going to argue with it.

There seems to be something built into us that hungers for stories. It's built into our genes. There are theories that state that stories are the way the human race survived over the millennia, over the eons, and we were able to pass down wisdom through our stories.

The Importance of Stories

Good stories are like telegrams in a way. Just like a telegram, stories condense a lot of information quickly.

When you use a story in selling, it has a very powerful effect. It gets across information and conviction. It makes implications so that people are more open to what you have to say. Stories are indirect but very powerful and concentrated.

Stories are not just good for reminiscing. They are also very helpful in helping people get to know you pretty quickly. In business, that's important because people like to do business with people they are comfortable with. One of the main reasons people don't trust other people is simply because they don't know them yet. So, stories are a real short-cut.

Story Type #1: "The Herald"

You know what a herald is. A herald is a person whose job is sort of like a reporter or a town crier. A herald is a person whose idea is to spread news. And, "The Herald" story is a story that introduces a new idea to a market that is unfamiliar with it.

A lot of times when you are selling something, you may have something that is new. You have a new idea. If you do, then this kind of story is going to work infinitely better than just laying out the facts.

A lot of people have a problem when they have something new to introduce to the market. Their problem is that they have spent so much time with it that they have forgotten how new it is. They have forgotten where their prospects are in their own mental awareness.

So it's very important when you use a story like this to realize, if you have something new that no one has ever heard of, you have to start with something that they are familiar with. This might not be your product. Then, you have to lead them into the discovery of your product with your story.

I have come up with an imaginary product. If this were a real product that someone has, great. But, let me just tell you the story.

> When people first started using Google Ad Words, it was a mixed blessing. On one hand, suddenly, here was a way to test whether or not you could sell something on the web and you would have bottom-line results in less than a day, sometimes within an hour or two.
>
> On the other hand, because it was possible to run so many Google ads at the same time, testing and tracking became a living nightmare. It seemed like you needed a Masters degree in computer programming and a PhD in statistics to be able to zero in on which ad worked with the best copy.
>
> But, this problem became a great opportunity for the few who could actually track and test with pinpoint accuracy. So, we decided it was time to create Ad Words Gazillions. We found a friendly but reclusive computer geek in Cawker City, Kansas, a

> town with under 1,000 people, "Home of the World's Largest Ball of Twine."
>
> He came up with the most ingenious solution. You simply install a piece of code on every selling page you are going to test and then, you use a special code in the URL of every ad words ad you run. And at the end of the day, you will have a profit-and-loss statement for each ad, to the penny, that you can import into QuickBooks or Excel.

Sounds useful. Did you get so wrapped up in the story that you didn't see what I was doing? That's okay. That's the way it's supposed to be. Stories actually get you so enraptured and focused that you don't really see the structure.

Here are the steps:

1. This was the situation.
2. Here was the problem.
3. Here was why it was hard or impossible to solve the problem before.
4. Here is what we came up with.
5. Here is how what we came up with makes it easier to solve the problem.
6. Here are the results people are having with our new solution.

Key Point:

A story cuts through the resistance of unfamiliarity like a white-hot knife cuts through soft butter. And unfamiliarity is the biggest form of resistance you have to deal with when you're introducing a new concept, or a new product or service based upon a new concept.

Story Type #2: "The Dissolver"

This template is used to answer prospects objections and dissolve them. I have to credit Mark Victor Hansen with this idea. I learned it from him at a Jim Rohn seminar a number of years ago. One thing he said always stuck in my mind.

Of course, he has used stories not to answer objections, but to sell 80 million books. But, he had stories on the brain, nevertheless. Maybe he still uses them to answer objections. It was a great idea.

Stories do answer objections very well. When somebody gives you an objection, when you are trying to sell somebody something, whether it's in print, in email, on the web or in person, objections usually boil down to one or more forms of disbelief.

Maybe they don't believe you are telling the truth. Maybe they believe you are telling the truth, but they don't believe they can afford it. Maybe they don't believe they are going to get their money's worth. There is something they don't believe that if they did believe, your whole sales situation would change very rapidly. They would say yes.

All objections boil down to one or more forms of disbelief.

And, if you can identify what that disbelief is, you can build a story that provides evidence of their belief to the contrary.

I really insist that these be true stories because I don't want you to get in trouble and it doesn't work very well if it's not true. Then you can turn that person from a disbeliever into a believer.

The purpose of "The Dissolver" is to answer prospects' objections and render them neutral and harmless.

Here is an example:

> Jeanine had a lovely white silk blouse she wore to a special anniversary celebration dinner with her husband.
>
> They ordered a very expensive California Cabernet and wouldn't you know it, just as Jeanine was taking a sip of this rare and delicious wine from a full glass, a pushy and clumsy older woman who was leaving the restaurant stupidly stumbled head-on into Jeanine... like a big, rambling Humvee barging through rush hour traffic.
>
> Wine went everywhere, including down Jeanine's white silk blouse.
>
> "I never thought I'd get it clean," she told us, "but WineAway worked just the way you said it would! And it didn't weaken or alter the delicate fabric one little bit."
>
> And while the accident ruined the dinner, WineAway saved the blouse.
>
> But Jeanine didn't mind too much because the owner of the restaurant invited Jeanine and her husband back for a second romantic dinner - on the house!

Here is the formula:

1. This problem occurred.
2. Someone thought they could never solve the problem.
3. They used your product.
4. They got these great results.

With stories, you want to take your prospect into a different world than the one they are in and excite their imagination.

The six words that will rivet the attention of anyone who reads or hears them are, "Let me tell you a story." Every time someone tells you about something that happened, you've just been told a story.

The key to making stories work is making them lively and relevant to what your reader is interested in.

Use visual descriptions. Use dialogue, instead of paraphrasing what someone said. Describe feelings, both positive and negative ones.

And don't forget about beginning, middle and end. Some people begin halfway through their stories, so you have no idea what they're talking about. Other people get off-track and never finish the tale.

Did you know that the world's most successful advertisement of all time, which has brought in over $2 billion in sales, is the Wall Street Journal's "Two Young Men" letter?

It begins, "On a beautiful late spring afternoon, twenty-five years ago, two young men graduated from the same college. They were very much alike, these two young men... "

The late Joseph Campbell, author of *The Hero With A Thousand*

Faces, said we all hunger for stories. My friend and screenwriting teacher Jim Bonnett says much the same. So when you tell a story in your copy, you are feeding a constant need that your prospect has.

There are other reasons, too:

People learn through stories, usually better and more quickly than they learn through the presentation of facts. If you want (or need) your prospect to learn about the unique benefits of your business, a believable story is the most efficient and effective way to do it.

People identify with the people you write or talk about in your stories. By getting mentally and emotionally involved with the people in the story, people are much more likely to take action on what they read next in the copy.

A story is the most direct route to another person's unconscious mind. Stories stir up fears and desires much more reliably than statements of fact, claims of benefit or empty, hollow phrases — all of which you see far too often in copy that doesn't work very well.

9

NASHVILLE, MEET COPYWRITING

Negative Optism–what is that? It's a term I invented with Armand Morin. Actually, Armand invented it for my technique. It has nothing to do with opt-in lists. It has nothing to do with optimism. Negative Optism is *the optimal use of negative thinking in your copy*.

There is a paradox here. If you are in sales, and especially if you are in business for yourself, there is a tendency to banish negative thoughts. As you know, this world is drowning in negative thought. We have to be positive in order to have the courage to break through, keep going, keep the business going, deal with the frustrations, and to deal with all of the relatives who say, "David, why don't you just get a job?"

A lot of us have trained ourselves to banish negative thinking from our minds. Here is the paradox. Your prospect is negative.

By negative, I don't mean they're bad. They have some negativity going on in their mindset or you need to stir some up. They may have suppressed it.

All copy boils down to something that is either going to solve the problem or help someone get something they want. The very fact that someone has a problem puts them in a negative state of mind. Even the most positive thinking people, if they're not Pollyanna's or totally in denial, do experience negative feelings sometimes.

Negative Optism does something very interesting. It shows empathy, and it creates rapport with your prospect. If you tell them how bad things are in a very specific way they can understand and relate to, then they know you know how it is.

If you tell your prospect how bad things are in a way they can identify with and relate to, then they know that you know the way it really is because that is the way it really is for them.

I understand this is rather abstract, so let me get specific. If you show that you know how bad things are from their point of view, then they know that you know how things really are. That way they can trust you.

Let me give you an example of this so you can see. Let's say you have a moneymaking product. In your copy, you could write something like this. By the way, as you're reading this, I'd like you to notice how conversational this copy is. All of the little principles and ideas we have discussed are going to start to interweave and come together.

> You think you got problems. I'm sure you do. We all have

problems. But, I remember when all my credit cards had been canceled. I was so late on the rent I was sure I was going to be evicted. None of my friends wanted to talk to me on the phone because they were sure at some point in the conversation I would be hitting them up for money. And the IRS had frozen my bank account!

I know it's no fun and I remember how scary it was for me. Even though at the time I couldn't see my way out of the hole I had dug myself into, I want you to know that there is a way out. I found out what it is, and I'm going to share it with you.

Have you ever been in that situation in your life? Did it sound pretty real to you? Yes, because that was my situation. That is exactly what happened. So, if I have a moneymaking product that I'm going to be promoting for myself under my own name, or in someone else's voice, I use that copy because it is real.

Here are the steps:

1. Acknowledge what the prospect may be thinking or feeling. "You think you got problems. I'm sure you do. We all have problems. I remember ..."
2. Validate it by talking about your own experience or about someone else's experience.
3. Talk about how horrible the reality really is from your own personal experience, if possible. If you can't talk about it from your own personal experience, don't make something up. Find someone who had this experience, understand what it was, and talk about it from their point of view. Make this as real as possible.
4. If you thought copywriting was all B.S. and fantasy, now

is the time you're going to change your mind about that and start to realize that your own experience is some of the most valuable stuff that has ever happened in your life, even if you did not think it was so great at the time.
5. Talk about how hopeless and overwhelmed you felt.
6. Reveal that you found a solution.
7. Transition by promising to share your solution with your prospect.

The purpose of Negative Optism is to let your prospect know that you understand how they feel. When they hear this and they feel that way about you, they also say, "Well, if they've been through that level of crap in their life," what goes on in the mind is, "then they will understand my situation. They are okay. They weren't born with a silver spoon in their mouth, either."

It makes you seem like a real person to them. It makes you seem not like someone who is above them or someone who is distanced from them. It makes you feel closer. And this will definitely help establish a bond that will, ultimately, help you make more sales.

I have used this in copy that has made tens of thousands, hundreds of thousands, millions of dollars. So, it is not just a theory. This is how it really works.

The purpose of this Negative Optism of sympathy is to get your prospect to know that you understand how they feel.

A lot of people who write copy have forced themselves to be positive — to banish negative thoughts. Most of the time that's a good idea. But, one of the key rules of copywriting is to meet your prospect where they are.

There is really no other way to say this. Sometimes, the best prospects are just plain miserable — including yours. Negative Optism is a constructive way to deal with negativity in your copy.

10

PUSHING BUTTONS THAT HIT THE JACKPOT

Breakthrough Copywriting emotional triggers are basically ways of taking the ordinary text in your copy, after the headline and all they way through to the P.S., and reformatting it or pumping up the emotional energy. Not randomly, but for a specific purpose.

The main thing you want your copy to do is motivate someone to take action. There are going to be some emotional hurdles along the way. I was giving a seminar to some corporate people in Florida a while ago, and I had a little game I did with crystal balls. They were these gag crystal balls that you can get, and you can shake them up.

What I did was I took one of their ads and I rewrote it about as badly as I could. It was actually a good ad, and I wrote it badly. I started reading it out-loud. The first crystal ball was the affirmation crystal ball. It said, "You're terrific." "You've lost weight, haven't you?" "Wow! That color looks good on you."

I would read a line and they would read what the crystal ball said to me. I'd say, "That's what we want to hear when people read our copy."

The second one was called a financial advisor crystal ball, and this one came across as the money-obsessed mind. I would read a line and it would say, "Sell short." I would read another line and it would say, "Bear market ahead." I would read another line and it would say, "I wonder how the NASDAQ is today?" That's what's going on in most of your prospect's minds.

Here is the really bad news. The third one was called the sarcastic crystal ball. I said, "When you've got a prospect who's interested, this is what's going on in their mind." I read the first line, and it said, "So what?" I read another line and it said, "Oh yeah?" I read another line and it said, "Right…"

This is the hard truth about copywriting. The more interested they are — the more skeptical they're going to be. The higher their level of desire and excitement — the higher their level of resistance is. These Breakthrough Copywriting Emotional Triggers are going to show you ways of diverting that resistance, turning off the critical thinking, melting that resistance, and transferring the energy from negative to positive.

#1 – "Anger to Envy to Offer"

Everything you learned in Sunday school or shul, or wherever you had your spiritual, religious education, sort of gets turned upside down in copywriting. The seven deadly sins are some of our best friends.

Even if you're a practitioner or follower of new age religion, it doesn't get much better. Peace, love and harmony don't work real well as sales motivators. But anger and envy are terrific. This one is called "Anger To Envy To Offer." I'm not telling you the way I think it *should* be, I'm telling you the way it *is*.

Here's the psychology of this. Anger and jealousy are two of the most powerful motivators known to man. In fact, someone said to me that jealousy is fear of loss brought into the immediate present. Think about that. If you see someone else walking away with something you want, that's fear of loss right before your eyes.

Here's how to channel them into your copy to motivate your prospect. For each one of these, I've given an example of an eBook. You can use this for an information product, an eBook, for a service or for product.

This could be an eBook on auto repair.

> For most people, the only thing worse than going to the dentist is taking your car to the mechanic. At least the dentist warns you when he's going to hurt you and he does his best to numb the pain, but Mike Thompson is different.
>
> For Mike, going to the mechanic is never a big deal, because he's never been overcharged, and he always gets treated with a level of courtesy and respect that a king would expect. Does Mike know something you don't know? He probably does, and that's why I thought you'd be interested in his new eBook *Never Let Your Mechanic Intimidate You Again: How to Stay in Control and Save a Lot of Money with Every Auto Repair You Get from Now On.*

What's going on in this story?

First of all, I'm talking about a common situation about feeling intimidated, ripped off or taken advantage of by your car mechanic.

If that's ever happened to you, don't you start to get a little angry as you think about it?

Especially when they say it'll be done by 5:00, and it's not done. What I did was I made a statement that would arouse anger in my target market. If I had this book, you'd probably buy it right now, wouldn't you?

The second thing is that I made a contrasting statement about a positive aspect of the same situation. Here is the contrasting statement. "But Mike Thompson is different. For Mike, going to the mechanic is never a big deal because he's never been over-charged, and he always gets treated with a level of courtesy and respect that a king would expect."

Do you feel a little jealous of this guy? We've gone from anger, "That blankety-blank mechanic said it'd be ready at five and it's not done," to envy, "This other guy never has to put up with it," to offer, "And here's my offer." "Does Mike know something that you don't know? He probably does, and that's why I thought you'd be interested in this new eBook, Never Let Your Mechanic Intimidate You Again."

To do this, make a statement that your prospect or reader can identify with about a negative situation that gets them angry, but not in a way that gets them angry with you. It gets them angry at the situation. You don't want to pick a fight with them.

You want to come in sort of sideways and let their remembering of that situation be a burr in their side.

What this does is help people realize they have a problem which you need to do if you're going to help them solve the problem. Then, make a contrasting statement about the positive aspect of the same situation that is likely to cause envy in your reader.

This stirs a lot of emotions. The emotions want to go somewhere, and where they can go is right into accepting your offer. You have to figure out what are people angry about that your product can fix. And the, work backwards from the problem your product solves. It's a pretty sophisticated strategy. Even though it's only three paragraphs, it may take a little think-through.

#2 – "Empathy Through Shared Misery"

The second one is "Empathy Through Shared Misery." Isn't this a fun thing? Anger... envy... misery... it's kind of like being married, isn't it? That's why I'm single, I guess… Here's the psychology of this one. You bond with your reader when you show them you know what they're going through.

Here's a way to bond that makes them much more comfortable considering your offer and buying. Speaking of being married, how about not being married? How about dating — a dating manual for guys?

> Have you ever walked up to a beautiful woman and watched helplessly as your lips turned to Jello? Don't feel bad. It's happened to a lot of guys. The problem is, when we were

> growing up, no one gave us instructions that really worked on how to go out with the woman of your dreams, until now.

Again, the neat thing about this stuff is, it slips in under the radar. It doesn't say, "New, fantastic, powerful." It just says, "Has this ever happened to you? It's happened to a lot of people." It sounds just the way people talk and here are the steps.

The first step is use an example to illustrate an important point that deals with a commonly experienced human emotion like misery, or a specific kind of loss, pain, grief or embarrassment. Notice, you don't have to really pump it up.

Notice that there are universal up-words. There are picture words here. "Lips turn to Jello." Everyone knows what Jello is, and everyone knows what it's like when you can't get the words you want to say out of your mouth.

Then, there's empathy. "Don't feel bad. It's happened to a lot of guys."

Then, you show compassion. And then, you show a way to eliminate the misery. "The problem is, when we were growing up, no one gave us instructions on how to go out with the woman of your dreams, until now."

From there, you can go right into the offer. It's very innocuous because it doesn't feel like anyone is trying to sell you anything. Obviously, it's a sales pitch, but it feels very conversational.

Those are the steps. Where do you use this? You use this when you want to get your reader to identify very personally with the issues that make them want and need your product. This is especially valuable right at the beginning, or after you've been talking about benefits, or more factual, technical types of things.

When you start to get into the logical mind, you are getting closer to critical thinking. You want to swing it back to that personal, emotional, right-brain, mid-brain, unconscious type of connection. This will pull them right back in.

#3 – "Doubt to Confidence"

Number three is "Doubt to Confidence." This is really important, because you know if they're interested, they're going to start to doubt that it's for real.

I once tried to get my mother to try some supplements. My mother was pretty conservative medically and believed in the old medical model. Even though the creator of the product was an M.D., he had some pretty new ideas. I sent my mother to his website and asked if she would take a look. She said, "No. It looks to good to be true. I won't even try it."

When I offered to get her a bottle, her response was, "No, I'll go to my doctor at Kaiser."

While she may not have been in the target market for this particular product, this often can be a problem for people who are in your target market. Sometimes, people don't have the level of confidence they need in order for you to get the maximum amount of sales.

Here's a very easy way to take care of this. You do it through using a testimonial that's structured in a particular way. Let's talk about an eBook for marketing professional services. This is a quote from anybody. This would be like a peer testimonial from someone who might actually be like a customer.

> Professionals have an especially thorny problem when it comes to marketing because often the kind of marketing likely to work is deemed too aggressive. On top of that, ethical standards often stand in the way of getting results from ads and mailings. When I started to read Never-Empty Waiting Room, I wondered if it would have the same [tepid] techniques I've read about so many times before.

There is the doubt.

Here is the confidence.

> It turns out my fears were groundless. The go-for-it methods mentioned in this book…

We are starting out with the thoughts in the readers' minds, and then we are putting them in the mouth of someone they can really identify with, as a testimonial.

We are taking that person through the transformation to confidence. People will respond to something where someone else is mirroring their own experience by going through that same emotional path themselves.

Testimonials can be very effective in sales letters. Consistently and constantly gathering testimonials should be a part of your business, if it isn't already. In order to get testimonials like these that take the prospect from doubt to confidence, you will need to poke and prod your customer base to get them. Often, you will have to drill down with your customer to get them.

When you ask someone for a testimonial, find out from them what specific results they are getting. Ask them to think back to when they read your copy. Was it hard for them to believe at the time?

Gathering testimonials is very important for any business owner. And, the more testimonials you can get that specifically address the doubt the person had when they first read the copy and the specific results they have achieved from using your product or service, the more powerful those testimonials will be.

#4 - "Appeal To People's Sense Of Larceny"

Now, you might think that good people don't have larcenous intentions, but everyone's got a little bit of a bargain hunter bordering on kleptomaniac in them.

Some people just call it "getting good value for your money." Some people call it, "I never pay retail." Some people call it, "getting the best price." Whatever they call it, people have it. The example's an eBook, but you can laterally transfer this to whatever your situation is.

> Career counseling is expensive, but often well worth it, especially in an employers' market where jobs are scarce, and applicants are plentiful. But cost doesn't have to be a concern of yours because *How To Find a Job When No One's Hiring* tells you how to get expert advice, custom tailored to your situation.

> Best of all, unlike other people going for the same job you are, who didn't even try to get counseling because they didn't want to shell out the money, you'll learn how to get this advice free without paying a penny of the career counselor's high hourly fees.

With this trigger, we create a problem — we create something that they can't afford. Career counselors can cost up to $200 an hour. The good ones probably charge more. Then we tell them, "Wait a minute, you don't have to pay that because you can get the same advice here." And then you say, "And you're going to beat out the other guy for the job because you'll have the advice because they were too cheap or they didn't have the money to buy it."

All in three paragraphs. Again, the reason this stuff is so effective emotionally is because it pushes buttons that most people don't push in the sales copy and it's not really hyperbolic or directly aggressive.

The steps are to point out something that your reader wants that is expensive, but they would rather not pay for. The whole idea is champagne taste on a beer budget. Works every time.

You point out something your reader wants that is expensive, but would rather not pay for and then you show them how they can "get away with getting this desirable thing without paying for it or paying a lot less for it and benefit from having it." Where do you want to do this? Before you announce your price. So, if you're selling electrons or you're selling an eBook for $100, but you just saved the person $2,500, what's $100?

#5 – "Emotional Math"

I learned about this from Gene Schwartz, but I have a slightly different spin on it. He talks about emotional math. His example is the old Avis slogan, "We're Number Two. We Try Harder." But he didn't really explain how to put it together. I will. This is an ingenious technique because it leaves a prospect to answer their own objections at an unconscious level. Not only to get your prospect to answer their own objections, but to do it without even realizing that there was an objection.

Once the objections are answered, the path is clear for action. Let's use this for an eBook on using the Internet to do detective work.

> Our software lets you conduct your own private eye investigation legally, anonymously and usually for no cost at all.

This sounds like a benefit statement, but there's more to it than that.

You say conduct your own online, private eye investigation and the devil, like the devil crow—the Heckle and Jeckle crow—says "Oh, yeah, I'm going to find out everything. This is really neat. Wow, I'm going to get the goods on him." And the angel crow on the other shoulder says, "Oh, but is it legal and will people know I'm doing it? Will it cost me a lot?"

All these things are going on, probably so fast, that unless you've trained yourself to listen to your unconscious, you wouldn't even know it. What you do is you answer it without ever bringing it up because you know it's also going to be reflexive because of the conflict the person is having. And you say it legally, anonymously and for the lowest possible cost.

Here's how you do it. You make a statement. Then you figure out what your prospect's reaction would be, but you never say anything about it. You just know what it is. You might want to write it out for your own notes. And, you immediately go from the statement you just made right to the statement that answers the objection that you never stated.

It's easy to do and, as you can see, it doesn't look like you're really doing anything except stating benefits. Again, you're getting in under the radar. Very important. Where do you use this? Use it anywhere in your copy, in your headline, in your positioning, near your close, in your P.S. The one thing you do not want to do is throw it somewhere in the middle of a paragraph, in the middle of a list of bullet points.

You want to use this prominently because people are skim-reading. You want to make sure that they catch this early on because this will immediately get them emotionally hooked and interested.

#6 – "Sour Grapes to Vintage Wine"

The next Breakthrough Copywriting trigger is called, "Sour Grapes to Vintage Wine." This one is sort of subtle. You know that when you're writing copy, you have to make a big claim. If you're introducing a new orange juice, you can't say, "This tastes about 1% better than the orange juice you're drinking now." You have to say something like, "This tastes much better." But here's the problem.

You have to do that, and yet, there's some people that when you make a big claim, especially if the claim involves how it's going to improve their life, they're going to go, "Nah. That wouldn't work... I couldn't do that. I mean, I'm not that..." and they will, for their own programming reasons, have blocks that will not allow them to imagine themselves in the optimum "after" situation.

I'll give you an example. A long time ago, I heard a story about Joe Karbo. He was running ads to recruit real estate people in the Los Angeles area (this was back in the '70s). He used the headline, "Make $50,000 A Year In Real Estate," and they got a moderate response. $50,000 was a lot of money then. I'm thinking maybe $200,000, $300,000, or $400,000 today. They revised the headline and said; "Make $20,000 A Year In Real Estate," and the phone rang off the hook because people believed they could do that smaller amount. That's the sour grapes idea.

Let me give you an example for an eBook on bodybuilding copy.

> Some people have told me they don't believe they can add 50 pounds to their bench press in a month. You know what I told them? They're right, because they look like sane people to me. "Well, I'm a sane person, I'm not crazy." You know what I told them?
>
> They're right because they look like sane people to me and the people who use what I teach to add 50 pounds in one month are usually the slightly insane body-builder types. But so what?

> "With what I can show you, you can easily add 20 pounds a month, every month. And I'll show you how to bench press so the gains you make in muscle mass and strength far exceed what you would have experienced by bench pressing 20 more pounds the way you were doing it before.

This takes that whole group of diminished-expectation prospects, people who don't think that they can shoot for the moon that would rather grab a cobweb off the ceiling and includes them. It includes more people. The other person, the gonzo guy who's on human growth hormone and steroids and everything says, "Yeah, I am insane...," so everybody's happy. That's "Sour Grapes to Vintage Wine."

#7 - "Factual Format For Emotionally Provocative Language"

This one's really great. I think this is my favorite. I used to be a journalist and one of the neat things about journalism that I didn't realize until I went into business for myself, is we have a huge advantage as journalists. People are trained to accept what journalists and media say is true. Copywriters are conditioned to believe that what we're not saying is not true.

One of the interesting things that about the way the mind works is if you borrow the format from another medium, people will automatically turn to their conditioning for that medium. What that means is if you use something that looks more like journalism than copywriting, people will apply their rules for whether or not to believe it.

They will accept it as more true. And that's one reason for what we call "advertorials." Those are long copy ads that look a lot like articles. Just the physical layout makes it look more believable. Now, you still have to prove your case. And, you better be telling the truth in the most dramatic way possible or you could get in a lot of trouble in a lot of ways, but you're not fighting against as many barriers.

The way this works is you take a statement and half of it is an acceptable fact and the other half is something that looks factual but really provokes the emotions. I'll give you an example for an eBook on a new approach to investing in stocks.

> How to identify the hidden indicators that typically precede rallies and sell-offs. Missing these could cost you a lot of money or some big profit-taking opportunities.

On the face of that, it sounds pretty factual, right? But what is going on here is the first half is definitely factual, "How to identify the hidden indicators that typically precede rallies and sell-offs." There are probably indicators. There is probably a way to identify them. But the second half of the statement is actually going to stimulate greed and fear of loss like you wouldn't believe, without looking like it's doing that.

It doesn't say, "You'll make wads of money that will come raining down on your head." It doesn't say that. It just says, "Missing these could cost you a lot of money or big profit-taking opportunities." When people are thinking about it though, they are going to think that it is true. And maybe it is; maybe it isn't. The indicators might not give you the opportunity to cash in. But people will not think critically about this.

This is sort of a cause-and-effect kind of statement. The steps to making this work are you make a statement about your offer or a benefit or some aspect of what you're offering in logical, factual language, like "How to identify the hidden indicators that typically precede rallies and sell-offs." And then, you add a phrase at the end that sounds logical, but it contains emotional hot words to spark strong feelings in your prospect. "It could cost you a lot of money."

Especially since people know that there are these indicators. They are out there but they don't know what they are. They will believe that. This is very powerful. The best place to use this is not right away because at the beginning of your copy, you want to get the emotions rocking and rolling. You usually want to do that by qualifying people with stories, with testimonials and by putting the person into a future situation where they have your product or service. Use it later on in a bullet point list or somewhere else later in the copy.

#8 - "The Drip Irrigation Method To Change Belief To Disbelief"

Let's go to the next one, "The Drip Irrigation Method To Change Belief To Disbelief." Again, this slips under the radar. What you do here is you start out with something that is irrevocably true and you slowly transition, bit by bit, to what you want your prospect to believe.

If you transition them slowly this way, they will come to accept what you want them to accept as true. It's like putting the frog in a boiling pot of water. He jumps out. Put the frog in a cold pot of water and turn up the heat slowly and he stays in and becomes your dinner.

Here's an example from an eBook on succeeding as a single parent.

> One of the biggest dilemmas single parents face concerns dating and not only for logistical problems, like babysitters and sex and even finding time for a date; conscious single parents often feel they're in a 'damned if you do, damned if you don't' situation. On the one hand, they want to meet interesting, exciting people.
>
> On the other hand, they don't want to be with someone who's so on the edge, that this person would have a bad influence on their kids. Maybe you've gone through this yourself. It's almost like you feel forced to lead a double life: your stable, responsible, family life as best you can manage it and your exciting, romantic, social life, if that's even possible.
>
> So, how do you reconcile these seemingly contradictory needs? What you have to do is find the right person who's both fun and a good influence on your kids. And the surprising good news is these people are more plentiful than you think.
>
> But how do you know in advance? It's simple, when you use the three good-for-me, good-for-my-kids questions. Asking and getting answers to these questions will tell you right away whether a potential date-mate is good news or bad news in the family room and in the bedroom. So, from now on, you'll start every relationship on the right foot or you won't start it at all.

It makes sense, right? It sounds pretty logical, right? But did you notice that the last sentence, "So from now on, you'll start every relationship on the right foot or not at all" is a huge leap, especially to a single parent in that situation. What we've done is we've made a series of statements that are true and have gradually transitioned from what they know to be true to what we want them to think is true. Here's how we did it.

Number one, you make an indisputably, true statement. "One of the biggest dilemmas single parents face concerns dating." Well, it's going to be true for your prospect. Then, you use this "drip irrigation," you drip a series of also absolutely true statements prospects can agree with, problems like babysitters, sex, finding time for a date. On one hand they want to meet. On the other hand, they don't want to meet.

And then you make a statement that blurs the line between what your prospect would unthinkingly accept as true and what they might think needs a little more scrutiny. "Finding the right person who's both fun and a good influence on your kids are more plentiful than you think."

And then you make your flat-out claim. "So from now on you'll start every relationship on the right foot." And all of a sudden, the prospect is convinced that you have solved a big problem for them and they somehow believe it is true. They really don't know what happened.

Where I went from the facts that they accepted as indisputably true to having them accept the truth I want them to believe is with the statement, "And the surprising good news is these people are more plentiful than you think." Well, there's absolutely no reason for that to be true.

I mean, I might know that to be true, but there's no reason for the prospect to believe that, except that I've been leading them up to it. I've been building credibility. The other thing is the word "surprising" is a trance word. When you use the word "surprise," it opens up the unconscious mind for just a little while.

#9 – "Emotional Downfall To Emotional Uplift"

This works in so many different contexts. One thing you have to understand is that people go through ups and downs emotionally when they are reading copy that appeals to them. If it appeals to them, they're not always going to be going, "Yeah."

They're going to run into brick walls. They're going to get upset. There are reasons: it could be price; it could be an objection that comes up; it could be that something you wrote reminded them of a bad experience.

You don't want to prevent them from ever feeling bad. You want to deal with it. It's sort of like you don't want to live where it never, ever rains. You want to own an umbrella. Let me show you how this one works because what "Emotional Downfall To Emotional Uplift" does is it turns the inevitable downs (negative emotions) into ups (positive ones). Let's talk about an eBook on losing weight quickly.

> If you've ever tried to lose weight in the past, you know how frustrating it can be. The hunger pangs, then the inevitable binges and all of your weight loss achievements are wiped out in one big orgy of overeating. Fortunately, you can put a stop to that cycle forever with the No-Brainer, No-Gainer Weight-Management Plan. You can easily lose all the weight you want and it stays off. Suddenly, what used to be a problem is now

> something that no longer concerns you. Eating is fun. Your clothes fit. You're healthy and you can get on with your life.

Did you actually go through the emotions as I was reading this?

This is easy to do. I know some of the other things we've talked about were complicated, but this one is easy. All you have to do is make a negative-emotion-inducing statement, like "if you've tried to lose weight in the past, you know how frustrating it can be."

Then you describe it. Follow with a series of positive assertions. "Put a stop to the cycle and lose the weight. It stays off. What used to be a problem is no longer a problem. Fun, clothes fit." And then make your assertion, "You can get on with your life."

Where do you want to use this?

The best place is anywhere people are likely to be skeptical or especially negative, hostile, or suspicious. In your copy, there are times when it's necessary to do things that are going to bring them down, or at least might bring them down, when you're explaining the work that the prospect must do to achieve what they want.

Of course, you don't want to over-emphasize that, but sometimes you need to disclose some of those things. When you give a technical explanation, technical explanations do not get people excited. This is especially important for software people and anyone doing something technical. No matter how excited they get, even a technical customer will not get excited from a technical explanation.

I was speaking at a seminar for a very technical company that sells very high-end scientific meters that cost thousands of dollars. I asked their copywriters if they talked to their customers. They said, "Well, we do have a CD each month where in our VP interviews someone." I said, "No, I'm talking about talking to your customers."

I said, "Look, is there anyone in this room who actually was a customer of this company at one point?" This one very shy woman raises her hand. I said, "That's great. What do you do?" She said, "I was a PhD research chemist." I said, "Okay. Could you talk about when you got one of these meters and what it was like?" She said, "I like to put my hands on it and I like the way they look." She was really embarrassed.

It was like a guy talking about running a new sports car through the countryside. It was exactly that kind of explanation. No one in that room had a clue about that. Of course, they would have to give them lots and lots of technical specs because they're selling technical products.

Can you see that someone who likes to put their hands on it and likes to look at it is going to get a little depressed when they're just reading all the technical specs and they're not getting to have those endorphins going through their body that they get from touching it or imagining touching it? That's why technical stuff does not really do the trick for people.

This is pretty easy to use. You can use it when you're explaining technical stuff. When you put your reader in pain to make them realize what they need to have, my advice is not to soft-pedal negatives, but instead be straightforward and direct. People will appreciate the honesty. But use a technique like this to bring them up.

#10 - "Shared Outrage"

This is a little different from "Anger To Envy To Offer." This is where both you and the reader are both really pissed off about something. When this happens — use it.

Let's talk about losing weight again. I'll give you a quick example.

> You know what it's like when diets don't work. It sucks. I remember one so-called 'diet' I went on. What a load of crap! I had stomach pains for weeks! I didn't sleep well, I was crabby and tired all the time, and at the end of five weeks I'd gained five pounds! I was so mad I wanted to smash something into a thousand little pieces.
>
> It was then that I made myself a solemn promise—never go through that humiliation again! I wanted a way to lose weight that was easy and permanent. I searched and searched until I had all the pieces in place for the perfect program—the No-brainer, No-gainer Weight Management Plan. And now I'm ready to share it with you.

Where's the order form? I'm ready to buy. It's just that powerful.

Here are the steps — you express your anger that the situation involving something you are upset about with your competitors, with the rest of the world, with the alternatives, and with the current reality.

"Diets don't work. It sucks. I'm crabby and tired. And after all that, I gained five pounds!"

That's anger, and people can relate to that anger. But you're not angry at them; you're angry at the same thing they're angry at.

The second thing is to use the anger as a springboard. Anger can be a tremendous springboard towards productivity, focus, and action if you use it in the right way. It can also lead to depression and confusion if you use it in the wrong way. You have to direct it. You direct it towards searching for a solution, coming up with a solution, using the solution, trying it out, and then offering it to your customer.

#11 - "From Desperation to Salvation"

Now you can have positive emotions. If you did love somebody, and you did want to get a blessing in your life, you'd want to give them a blessing that you came up with and that you found worked for you. Wouldn't you? Yes. It's the whole range of emotion. It's like the bass notes on the guitar and the high notes. They're all there.

This one comes across as religious and I think it's a good religious marketing technique, but it will work for anyone. It is "From Desperation To Salvation."

Desperation is a very powerful emotion because it begs salvation. Desperation is an impatient wanting and it's desperate. When you use this trigger, you provide salvation and they can't wait to get it themselves.

Let's talk about an eBook on free groceries. It starts out like this:

> Too much month at the end of your money. Do you know that one? It's been a problem in our family since forever. We did our

> best by economizing, but those commercials! The kids want all the latest cereals, toaster goop (that's what I call stuff like Pop Tarts) and anything else they saw on TV. It was a real headache!
>
> I wouldn't stop them from watching TV because then they'd never shut up about it. I had to drag them with me when we went shopping and they still keep trying to fill my shopping cart with all that stuff we can't afford. I don't know what I would have done without the life-saving secrets I learned in Free Groceries: Stretch Your Food Dollar By Not Spending It in the First Place. Now we save so much money at the store each month, I can get whatever extras and treats that I want.

Here is how you do it. You put someone like yourself, your reader, or a third party in a situation of desperation where you desperately need something. "We did our best by economizing, but the kids wanted everything they saw on TV."

You increase the desperation level by making what they need almost impossible to find. "They kept trying to fill my shopping cart with stuff we couldn't afford." You then save the day by bringing in your product. Your product is the hero of this drama. You deliver salvation in this way. Your product provides a solution to your reader's problem. It's a solution that, as far as they or you are concerned, didn't even exist and couldn't possibly exist.

That's "From Desperation to Salvation." It's very powerful. Where do you use it? Use it any place where you have to overcome inertia. This is not where people get skeptical. This is where people go, "I don't know if I want to buy it or not." This is where they're stuck in "Copywriting Junction" at the intersection of "Maybe." (See beginning of Chapter 1).

You put it at the beginning of your copy, maybe after the first 300 words or so, where they decide if they're going to keep reading or not. You can put it right before you launch into a long list of bulleted benefits. This will really send them into that list. You can put it a little while after you've announced the price where they're thinking, "I don't know if I want to spend that kind of money or not."

Finally, you put it in the P.S., where the reader who may be wavering about buying could use just a little push to make the purchase.

11

THE SECRET THAT WORKS EVERY TIME

DNA is the little collection of chromosomes in the double helix. It's the technical thing that pretty much determines your features, your anatomy, your facial features, your metabolism, and your appearance. DNA here is, of course, a metaphor. There is a certain DNA for the copy that has been Babe Ruth-like and Barry Bonds-like, that not only hit home runs, but also hit the ball out of the park and broke all records. There are certain themes.

We've gone into a lot of detail, and this is more of the big picture. If you have your own mental camera, I want you to not think of the close-up, but step back into the big picture.

What we're going to do now is look at the themes of the biggest winners in copywriting history. Not only what are those themes, but also how can you use those themes in your copy.

Sometimes people question whether the "old stuff" still works.

Human nature hasn't changed and won't change, and human psychology hasn't changed. Copywriting themes that have worked decades ago are working now.

The media or delivery format may have changed, but we as human beings have not.

Breakthrough Copywriting DNA is these themes. The way you would use it is by building your copy around the themes that we are going to talk about.

#1 - "From Humiliating Defeat to Triumphant Victory"

The first one is called "From Humiliating Defeat To Triumphant Victory." If these start to look like themes of movies, stories, Bible stories, legends, or themes of fairy tales, that's not a coincidence. These are themes of stories that inspire people. These are stories, and I hope by now you see that copy is a story and that you're telling a story. It may not be a true story, but it's a story. It's not just a series of bullet points.

There are certain stories that we crave to hear and that are important to us as part of the inspiration of our life. Let me tell you a story. Let me take you back to the 1920's to Coney Island in Brooklyn. It's summer, and the sun is hot. You're on the beach. The sand is hot beneath your feet, and the breeze is cool. You hear the hot dog vendors. You can smell all of the foods. The waves are rolling in.

Off in the distance, you see a young man lying on the beach on a beach towel. It's a real skinny guy with his girlfriend. This big hulk of a bully comes up and kicks sand in his face. He shudders and his girlfriend says, "What are you going to do about it?" He says, "Nothing." He's looking at this bully. The bully laughs at him. He makes fun of him and walks off. The girlfriend leaves. She doesn't really want to be with a guy who's not going to protect her.

Flash-forward a year. It's the same beach and the same people, except now the guy is pretty ripped and built up. The bully comes up and says, "There's that little squirt again," and he kicks him. The same guy gets up, and he beats the living crap out of the bully. His girlfriend is all over him. I am going to stop the story there, even though we are all adults here. You can imagine the rest.

Do you recognize that story? That story has been running as a comic strip for 70 years. A copywriter named Charles Roman wrote it about an Italian immigrant. He was from Acri in Calabria, and his name was Angelo Siciliano. Angelo came over to the United States. That actually happened to him. He built himself up, and it didn't happen to him anymore.

Charles Roman was a Manhattan copywriter. The name of the comic strip was "The Insult That Made a Man Out of Mac; From Humiliation to Victory." The product was the Charles Atlas Dynamic Tension Course. For 70 to 80 years, that story keeps going.

Here's another story. It's about a guy who used to work 80 to 100 hours a week. He would have to beg the bank to lend him money because he was not making enough money. Now, he only works 30, 34, and 40 hour weeks. He has several homes and he lends the bank money, $50,000 at a clip.

Who am I talking about? Joe Karbo – creator of the Lazy Man's Way to Riches. He couldn't run enough of these ads. He ran them in newspapers all over the country to sell a little $10 book. Of course, a $10 book today might be $30 or $40.

So, that is a theme. Do you understand how that is a piece of DNA you can put in your copy? It has to be credible and relevant. The steps are you start out with a story of humiliation like getting beat up in front of your girlfriend at the beach, or working hard and still having to borrow money and being held in low esteem by your bank. You tell how you solved the problem and then you show the reader how they can solve the problem, too.

#2 - "The Secret Formula For Success & Prestige"

The next one is "The Secret Formula for Success & Prestige." You've probably heard about The Wall Street Journal letter. It is considered to be the ad that has made the most money in the history of advertising. It's somewhere between one and two billion dollars.

You have probably gotten this letter; it's been running for about 23 years now. It starts on a beautiful spring day in June… I'm not going to quote it exactly; it's copyrighted anyway, so I can't — two young men graduated from college. They have the same grades and they're similar guys. It takes you through their careers, and then they meet at a class reunion 25 years later. They both work for the same company.

One was the president, and one was a manager working for the president. The difference was that the president read The Wall Street Journal. Then, they talk about The Wall Street Journal and they say, "While we can't guarantee your business success, what we can promise you is…" At the end, they have a little "P.S."

that says, "Your subscription may be tax deductible; ask your accountant." That letter has made more money than anything. "The Secret Formula for Success and Prestige" — it's interesting, isn't it?

#3 - "Your Unrecognized Greatness Has Been Discovered"

The next one is called, "Your Unrecognized Greatness Has Been Discovered." This one is interesting because it relates a lot to the talk about the subconscious mind.

Is the subconscious mind different from the super-conscious, or your spiritual self, or your connection to a larger, greater oneness? I don't know. I do know that at some deep level, people know that they are more than they have been acknowledged for in the world. People know that there is greatness inside them that it is generally not recognized.

When you have a DNA theme in your copy that shows them that in a direct — or even better, in an indirect way that implies their greatness — sales can go through the roof.

One example is the Halbert *Coat-of-Arms* letter.

Gary Halbert has been a great influence on me. He was a very controversial and provocative guy. The first letter he wrote was a little letter. It would say something like, "Dear John, in doing some genealogical research, we recently found that there is a coat-of-arms for the MacDonald family. If you…"

"If you would like to have a copy of it, we would be glad to send it to you for free. Just send us $3 for postage and handling." This letter had been mailed at least 600 million times, more than once to each American and probably in other countries, too.

The reason I believe this worked is that there is an implication. What does a coat-of-arms imply? In Europe, it means royalty or nobility. There is a tradition in Europe that the royalty and nobility have almost a divine or God-given right above other mortals, which is implying that there is a divinity to a person — a defined quality to a person whose family has a coat of arms. It's very subtle. It's not explicit. But this is the conclusion that the reader comes to in their mind.

The way this works is first you talk about the unique achievement status or other specialness that you're offer makes available to people. There are a lot of implications here, so let me go through that. A coat of arms offers recognition. It offers status. It's like a degree on the wall, a citation, an award, an Academy award, a trophy, or a world cup in a sense, about your genes.

You talk about that, and then you personalize that to your reader. There's nothing more personal that someone's last name and first name, the family name. Then, you show the reader how easy it is to accept your offer.

I'll give you another example. I've written an eBook with Jim Edwards, and I'm very good friends with Joe Vitale. We've done business together and been partners, as well. Jim and Joe partnered on a book called How to Write and Publish Your Own eBook in as Little as Seven Days. This book had been at the top of the ClickBank business-to-business list for a couple of years.

What is the implication in there? It just sounds like it's a how-to book on the surface, doesn't it? What kind of person would write an eBook? Watch all the causalities and all the implications here. What kind of person would write an eBook? Obviously, it would be a person that has something to say. What kind of person would have something to say? Somebody who's pretty important, somebody's who's great, and somebody who has unrecognized greatness. Just the very offer discovers that greatness. You're unrecognized greatness has been discovered.

Here are the steps for putting together Breakthrough Copywriting DNA strand number three.

1. Talk about the unique achievement, status or other specialties.

2. Personalize the greatness in your offer.

3. Show the reader how easy it is to achieve this.

#4 - "Free Little Known Wealth Building"

The next one is "Free Little Known Wealth Building"... I know this sounds like a Gary Halbert headline, but it's not. His would be a little more adrenaline inducing than this. This is a very specific strategy.

Here's an example: The first one was an ad written and published in 1948 for Merrill Lynch Pierce Fenner and Smith, which is now Merrill Lynch, the stockbrokerage firm. It was the kind of ad that ad agencies hate and copywriters love. It was over 6,000 words. The type was actually smaller than a regular newspaper type.

It ran in one New York paper. They offered a free booklet. They explained all about the stock and bond business. "What Everybody Ought To Know About This Stock And Bond Business" was the headline. The ad explained it in some detail and offered a free booklet. Not only did they get 5,000 responses, but 10% of them were for specific information about specific types of investments.

In sales, we call that a buying sign. When someone gets that specific, it's a buying sign. As a result, they ran this in over 500 papers around the country. That's unprecedented. Of course, it won't work anymore in that context and format, but the concept will, but that particular application won't. Merrill got an awful lot of business out of that ad.

#5 - "Only If You Qualify..."

Gary Bencivenga also used this when he put together his Bencivenga 100 seminar promotion. Gary Bencivenga said, "If you meet these four qualifications, you qualify to come to my seminar."

Do you want to know what the fourth one was? "Write me a check and send it to me when and how I tell you." He literally wrote that on his web page. You have to do it his way. This guy has really got all the buttons. There were four qualifications, which I respect by the way. I think it's great that someone has the *"Cojones"* to do that.

Of course, you have to have a desirable offer. Qualifying people is very powerful. If you've done your homework, you should be able to do this anyway. Qualifying is knowing who your customer is and who is not your customer. You should know that. Remember, if your market is everyone, then it's no one. So, you need to know who your market is. This is just telling them.

Start by telling who this is for and who this is not for. In qualifying, you want to disqualify. You want to tell people who it's not for. In a Frank Kern letter, I think he said, "This is going to offend a few people. Some people aren't going to like this." He just laid it right out there. Then, you tell your sales story. Then, before you close, you re-qualify.

#6 - "Turn Trash Into Cash"

Meg Whitman, former CEO of eBay, was named the most powerful woman in business by Fortune magazine years ago. EBay, of course, is the place where you can sell all the trash in your house to somebody else who wants to fill up their garage. This is an offer. There are eBay services when I go to my UPS store. There's a folder, somebody that has a concession or a joint-venture with them.

They offer, "If you don't want to sell it on eBay yourself, they'll sell it for you." This will give you a big clue into my personality. When I was about six years old, I was reading Popular Science magazine. There was this little ad about how you could grow earthworms in your backyard and then you could sell them. You don't even have to be a farmer; you just throw the worms in. The whole thing worked up until one point. I couldn't find anyone to buy them. But I did have a lot of worms.

So, that's "Turn Trash Into Cash. Have you ever seen those coin ads that say, "If you have a 1945 D nickel, it's worth..." People go through their coins. This is powerful. It's not for everybody.

Let me just tell you the steps.

1. Start with a big claim.
2. Prove with real life examples.
3. Show how your offer makes it easy for your reader to cash in on this.

#7 - "You Worked Hard And You Deserve A Reward"

Remember "You deserve a break today" — the old McDonald's theme? I assume that worked. McDonald's seems to be tracking the effectiveness of their advertising better than most corporate advertisers.

They've fallen into the coolness contest for advertising. I do remember when I saw the Clio Awards. Do you know what the Clio Awards are? That's where the advertising industry has their own little "Academy Awards." I was speaking at the Academy of Art College the next day in San Francisco. Coincidentally, the Clio Awards had been on the night before.

I was talking about advertising and the difference between the kind of copy we're talking about here and that kind of advertising. I said, "I was watching the Clio Awards last night and there was only one ad that actually was any good. It wasn't one of the winners. It was an actual ad between the parts of the show. It was a McDonald's ad and it really made me hungry."

There was this guy in the back and he was asleep. He stood up. I knew it affected him the way it affected me.

The Lazy Man's Way To Riches is another one, too. There's also the implication that the guy has worked really hard all his life, so he deserves an easier way to make all the money.

12

THE COMPLETE FORMULA

In this chapter, we will bring it all together. Often, people will ask, "Am I putting the bullets in the right place?" We all wonder those kinds of things.

The reality is, there is no right place. It just has to flow.

The best I can tell you is there are three ways to find out if it does. One is if you have a lot of experience, you will know. The second way is if you read it out loud and you start to trip over some of the words, you know it is not flowing there. And, the third way is if you show it to someone else and note that they criticize the grammar or that they have a problem with the spelling. But if they really don't understand or they just don't get it, then you know it's not flowing.

The way to fix this is to just turn it into a conversation based on everything you have learned and what we are going to talk about.

And yet, when it comes to how you put the whole thing together, I will continue to be honest and tell you that there is no one way. There are enough general rules and overall structures, so you don't have to worry about it.

I'm sorry if that seems like a little bit of a discouraging or confusing message.

It's really not. What it is saying is that there are some general rules that you can easily understand and then, things are just going to flow and come together the way they do. We are going to leave the "paint-by-numbers" approach here a little bit and take it more into the spontaneity of everyday conversation in life.

How Much Copy Do You Need?

The quick answer to "how much copy do you need" is the same answer that Abraham Lincoln gave when someone asked him how long a man's legs should be. He said, "Long enough to reach the ground." That's a pretty flip answer, I know. But, it's a good one.

In other words, the answer to how much copy you need is enough to get the person you are writing to, to take the action you want them to take. Understand that this action is not always to complete the sale. Sometimes, it is to get them to give you a call. Or, if it is in an Ezine or in Google AdWords, the action you want them to take is to click on the link.

So, remember that maybe the most important thing you want to think about before you really start writing is what action you want them to take.

From the prospect's point of view, it's another set of questions. You need to be able to answer both sets of questions before you really start writing.

How Do You Know It's Ready?

You will know that your copy is ready when it starts where the prospect is, and it takes them on a fairly complete path that is as efficient, enjoyable and interesting as possible. And enjoyable doesn't always mean pleasurable.

There could be some pain and some drama in the process. But, it gives them an emotionally interesting journey from where they are, to the point where they are ready to take the action you want them to take.

Five Main Things to Remember When You Put Your Copy Together

So, what I want to do is give you five things to think about when you put your copy together.

These things are going to be very useful to you. I could give you hundreds of rules, but I am just going to give you five. If you just keep these things in mind, it will really help your copy a lot.

The first one, and I got this from a book called *How to Write a Good Advertisement* by Victor Schwab. This is an extremely valuable book. You can get it on Amazon.

1. Start where your prospect is.

What that means is start with their state of mind, not yours.

Start with their problem, not with your product. And let them know you know how they feel.

This is an incredible challenge for all of us, because as we create our product we get so into the inside technical aspects, the process, and our own level of sophistication. It's almost like if life were a movie, you would have to reel backward to the point before you knew what you know and realize that is where your prospect is.

You have to reel backward to the point where you first had the problem that caused you to create the product, or you discovered a problem in others that caused you to create the product. And you have to start there. If there was an education or learning curve you went down, you have to repeat that. You can't just jump into where you are.

If you are serious about studying copywriting, I highly recommend *The Robert Collier Letter Book*. One of the things he said about copy, and I think he said this about headlines, is you want to enter the conversation that's already going on in your customer's mind.

Now, did you know that a conversation was already going on your customer's mind? Did you know that we're always having conversations in our mind? Aren't you answering my questions silently as I'm asking them? Yes, you are.

What you need to do is learn to anticipate that conversation and write like you're having a conversation. It is so important. Once you know how to do that, then this technique is very easy.

2. Remember this is a sales conversation.

Copy is a sales conversation. It is not a book report. It is not a term paper. It is not a white paper. It's not a newspaper article. It's not random word-salad. It's a sales conversation where there is an objective.

In doing this, you need to know where you are going. You have the tools to get there. But, there are some other things. In school and in the corporation if you work for the corporation and in the government if you work for the government, you have been taught to use big words, depersonalize things and be objective. This is not a sales conversation.

In a sales conversation, you want to use short words and two of the short words you want to use a lot are "you" and "me." You want it to be personal between you and the other person.

The other thing, and this is why I recommend *The National Enquirer* so strongly, you want your copy to have words that are emotional, that are visceral, physical, and that are visual. And *The National Enquirer* is full of words like that. Ordinary conversation is full of words like that. Country & Western songs are full of words like that.

Reports on the state of the economy from the Department of Commerce are bereft of words like that.

So, you want to make a sales conversation.

3. If you are not advancing the sale, you are diminishing the sale.

A number of years ago, I took a seminar at an airport hotel with Dan Kennedy. Dan put on this seminar and at the time he didn't realize how hard it was to get people in a room for a copywriting seminar. He only got four of us. It was one of the greatest seminars I ever took. I asked him a question. His answer was probably the most important thing I have learned about writing copy. See, I am a creative person. You may be creative, too. And there is a problem because you want to go off and tell jokes. You want to do something interesting. You want to do something with graphics, or you want to try haiku and all these different things, because you are creative, experimental and curious.

So, I said to Dan, "You don't want your copy to be boring, but how do you know when you are being too creative? Where do you draw the line on creativity?" And he gave me the best answer and this is it. "Does it advance the sale?"

It's a tough test. If you put every word and every sentence through that test, are you literally trying to close a sale? Or, are you trying to get a response? Collect a name? Get a phone call? Does it advance the sale?

Here is what advances the sale. Advancing the sale occurs when you provide information and stimulate feelings that lead the prospect to believe it is better to take the action you request than not to.

You might wonder what diminishes the sale. What diminishes the sale is everything else, including listing your credentials that don't directly apply to your product or service, entering information that leads the prospect's mind in another direction, and long dull lists of features where the benefits of those features to the prospect is not clearly and compellingly spelled out.

In sales, there is no middle ground. Either it is going up, or it is going down. Either you are moving forward, or you are moving backward.

Move forward.

4. Without proof, no sale.

You remember my friend, the copywriter Ted Cooper. He wrote great ads in the early days of Apple and Intuit. Ted said that every bit of copy basically needs to have three components:

1 - Make a claim.

2 - Prove it.

3 - Ask for action.

I have added a fourth component:

4 - Leave everything else out.

What facts to back up claims? Case studies, statistics, your own accomplishments - including especially how you've done what you promise you will do for other people or how others have done with your product, what you are telling the prospect they will be able to do, testimonials and logic.

What constitutes proof? Facts to back up claims, case studies, statistics, your own accomplishments, and these are accomplishments relevant to what your product offers, including especially how you've done what you promised you will do for others or how others have done with your product that you are telling the prospect they will be able to do themselves, testimonials and logic.

Understand that proof is not only a sales necessity; it's a legal necessity.

And it is going to be more important, not less as time goes on, because the FTC is going to be looking ever more closely at the Internet.

5. Make it very clear on how to take action and make it very easy to do so.

Finally, the fifth thing you need to remember is make it very clear on how to take action and make it very easy to do so.

Create the whole order form. Lay it out. Do the HTML. Test the Javascript, whatever you need to do. Get that crystal clear so it cannot screw up. Actually walk through the steps and find the bugs.

Search aggressively for bugs and get rid of them before you do anything else because here is why: anything that makes it hard or confusing to take action reduces sales.

13

HOW TO MAKE GOOD, EVEN BETTER

Often, marketers and entrepreneurs approach me to critique their copy. (If you'd like a critique, go to: www.garfinkelcoaching.com) The process I go through with my formal critique process is quite extensive. While each piece of copy is different, I have found several major mistakes that affect conversion rates come up often during my reviews.

I've listed some of the biggest mistakes here with the quickest way to fix these problems. That way, if your copy has any of these mistakes, you will be able to quickly adjust.

Mistake #1: Copy Has No Power & Doesn't Make Sense

If your copy has no power, it's not going to move people to action. Power is the ability to get things done.

I know power has a real bad name like "the abuse of power," "absolute power corrupts." That's not the kind of power I'm talking about. Here I'm talking about a more technical, neutral type of power. It's the power to get something to move from this point to this point.

When your copy has no power, it's not going to motivate someone. When it doesn't make sense, people will not buy or act when they're confused unless they're very afraid.

Mistake #2: Copy Doesn't Target The Ideal Prospect

To the reader, your copy feels like it was written for someone else. The biggest mistake most people make with their copy, after they know the basics of what to do, I would say is they don't really know their customers.

I'm lazy, so I just think of one question: what keeps them awake at night? Or, if they wake up and they're married, what are words are they going to say? "Honey, if we could only…then…" I think of just one sentence.

Mistake #3: Copy Looks Like A Book Report

When copy looks like a book report from school, it doesn't reach deep into your reader's heart, soul, and mind. You can't even do this unless you've taken care of number two. You have to know who the prospect is, because once you know who they are, you have to reach into them.

What is the single best way to reach into the reader's heart, soul, and mind? The answer: A story. Tell a story. When you're with a little kid and you open up your mouth to say, "Let me tell you a story," what happens? Their eyes dilate wide and they get glassy, and the listener goes into a trance.

Guess what — we're wired that way. It never leaves us. It still happens to us as adults. There are other ways, but the first way to start and the way that arouses the least suspicion in your reader is a story.

Mistake #4: Lifeless, Boring, or Forgettable

The fourth mistake is the copy if lifeless, boring, and totally forgettable. One of my favorite authors is David Ogilvy. In his typically British way, he said, "You can't bore people into buying." It's true; you can't. I guess occasionally there might have been a salesman who was so boring that somebody bought something just to get them out of their office.

But, it probably was not a real big-ticket item. On big-ticket items, they want to enjoy being with you and they want to enjoy being with what you're writing. If you don't think you're an interesting person, I have to tell you that you're wrong. You are – you just haven't discovered it yet. You haven't figured out how to do it. But, you have to put life energy into your copy whether it's a Google AdWords ad, or whether it's a 16 page sales letter, a podcasting script, or anything in between.

It has to be memorable. Now, memorable doesn't necessarily coming up with a slogan that becomes part of the pop culture, and becomes a meaning that goes into a Malcolm Gladwell description. I don't mean that. I just mean memorable. There are certain things you think about after you've read them.

Dan Kennedy was the person who experientially taught me the power of this. I'd get letters from him and would throw them in the trash. I couldn't leave them in the trash. I had to pull them out and read them again. Then, I would throw it away, and pull it out again. Then, I ended up ordering. That's memorable. That's what I mean by memorable.

Mistake #5: Copy That's Not Believable

Charles De Gaulle, the famous French General and President once said, "Since a politician never believes what he says, he is quite surprised to be taken at his word." Now, think about that for a second. Most of us don't believe most of what politicians say, and of course, maybe the politicians don't believe it either.

How does that apply to copywriting?

Well, very simply. If you don't believe in what you're trying to sell with your written word, it's going to come across and people won't believe it, either. If they don't believe it, they won't buy.

James Webb Young wrote *How to Be an Advertising Man,* which could be a man or a woman these days. In his *Diary of an Ad Man,* he said, "Every advertiser has the same problem; which is to be believed."

For your copy to be effective, you have got to believe in yourself and in what you say for your copy to be effective.

Quick Fixes

There are two ways to fix these five problems. Number one is to really understand who your customer is. Really understand how they feel. What they think. What their life is like.

When I say understand, I don't mean, "Well, they live in this zip code, so their income is about... They have between two and three kids." That is not understanding. Those are demographics and statistics.

I'm saying, what is the experience of their life like? When they get up in the morning, are they happy or are they sad? Are they pissed off about going to work, or are they thrilled because they're doing something they really love? How do they deal with frustration?

Do they understand, like I do, that frustration is part of the game? "I'm a quick study, but a slower learner, so I'm going to have to make every mistake in the book before I get it right. But, when I get it right, I'll really know what the right way is." Are they like that, or are they like I used to be when I had a job I really didn't like? Every little thing would make me hit the roof. What are they really like?

So, really understand who your customer is. The second thing that is going to solve those four problems for you is to really understand what your product, your service, or your information product is, what it does, and what it means to your customer.

There is a lot in that sentence, and I am differentiating the product from service from information products. Those are three different categories in my mind. A product is something physical. A service is something that gets delivered and is intangible. Information products are videos, audios, eBooks or any digitally delivered product and information products.

You have to understand what it is. What the components are. What it actually contains. And, what all the different aspects are. You have to understand it in the whole and in detail. Then, you have to understand what it does and what that means for your customer.

If you sell supplements, one of the things supplements do is increase your energy level. If you sell software, one of the things your software does is improve the person's golf game. If you sell an eBook about golf, it may do the same thing. That's what it does, but what does it mean?

It means where you really reach them in their souls. You really reach them in their hearts. You really reach them in their gut. Once you know these things, then all of the other stuff is going to work a lot better.

AFTERWORD

We've been through a journey together into the exciting (and challenging) world of copywriting. I hope by now you see how copywriting really is "the spoken language in written form."

Let me encourage you to put into practice what you learned in this book. It can make a huge difference in your career... your business... and, believe it or not, in your entire life.

It has for me, and for the men and women I have mentored in professional copywriting.

What could be more important than the ability to persuade others with what you write?

I suppose there are many things, but in my life, copywriting has made all the difference in the world.

I set out as a goal to make it as easy as possible for others to learn something that was indeed *very* hard for me to learn —

after a very successful first career as a professional writer (who didn't even know what copywriting was).

To the degree that I have succeeded, I am grateful. Please help me with my goal. Take what you have learned and let it flourish in your own life.

David Garfinkel
San Francisco

Be Sure to Check Out My Other Books:

Advertising Headlines That Make You Rich!

Copywriting Secrets for Infopreneurs (On Audible)

The Copywriter's Podcast

Each episode takes a "deep dive" into a narrow slice of copywriting--narrow, but something vitally important.

www.copywriterspodcast.com

Printed in Great
Britain
by Amazon

32207756R00088